"Kathryn and Clare have written the workbook to help you heal your pain. The tools you need to start navigating the emotional fall-out of losing your mate and getting your life back on track are embedded in these pages. Science shows that walking through your heartbreak with expert guides changes everything. We have all been right where you are and this workbook is a much needed resource. Clare and Kathryn have brought the process of healing into focus and action within this workbook. It will be a gem for many who are reeling after loss."

Dr. Sue Johnson (EdD), Founder of Emotionally Focused Therapy, Director of the International Center for Excellence in Emotionally Focused Therapy (ICEEFT)

"For all of us who have felt the agonizing pain of relationship betrayal and loss, this book by Kathryn D. Rheem and Clare Rosoman is a needed pathway for healing the wounded heart. My colleagues clearly understand the emotional devastation, confusion, and profound loneliness that can be unbearable when our hearts are broken. The chapters of this book guide the reader through the exact steps needed to heal from the deep pain of the heart and soul that comes with relationship loss. It is the same process I use with my clients in therapy. While expressed in culturally sensitive ways, your pain and my pain can be transformed when we can allow ourselves to feel and even befriend it. Rheem and Rosoman offer the reader a guided series of exercises designed to reduce the damaging spiral of emotional pain, heal the wounded heart, and revive the spirit toward growth. While this journey is not painless, you can trust the pain will shrink as you follow their masterful lead. They have written this book with clarity, empathy, and humanity. They are experts and knowledgeable guides, and you will hear yourself in their words and feel better as a result."

Dr. Paul T. Guillory (PhD), EFT Trainer, Author of Emotionally Focused Therapy with African American Couples: Love Heals

"Facing relationship loss is difficult and all the more so when done alone. This workbook meets you in the heart of loss, guides you through its painful uncertainties, and leads you toward a healing path of resilience and recovery. As compassionate companions, Drs. Rheem and Rosoman walk the journey with you with wisdom, kindness, and hope. Truly an exceptionally honest, inspiring, and practical resource for making it through the hurts that come in love and life."

Dr. James Furrow (PhD), Professor, Family Therapist and Contributing Author/ Editor of Becoming an Emotionally Focused Therapist, Emotionally Focused Family Therapy, and The Emotionally Focused Casebook

"Wow, finally an attachment book that helps us deal with the pain of losing connection. This invaluable resource will help so many people learn how to authentically face their loss and in the process transform it into growth and resilience."

George Faller, LMFT, EFT Trainer, Author, Co-Host of Foreplay Podcast, Founder of Success in Vulnerability

"If you are suffering from the heartbreak of a relationship loss, you will not want to be without the comfort and wisdom of this workbook. From the first pages, you will feel the authors' strong, caring presence. They draw on cutting edge attachment science and decades of clinical experience to walk you through your grief and confusion. You will be taken through a process that helps you make sense of your distress and reflect on your relationship, but the journey will feel uniquely personal because the authors do not assume all people are the same and process emotions in the same way. In the end, this workbook is about much more than healing a broken heart. It is about getting to know and befriend your emotional world so you can use its inherent wisdom to rebuild your life and love again."

Dr. Veronica Kallos-Lilly (PhD), ICEEFT Certified EFT Trainer, Co-Author of An Emotionally Focused Workbook for Couples: The Two of Us 2nd Ed.

T0373526

"I love this book. Most of us don't know how to move through the grief from losing a partner. Rheem and Rosoman get it and they want to walk with us as we heal from our losses. Their insights and understanding of the overwhelming pain of loss are deeply moving. This new workbook is insightful, accessible and very empowering."

Jette Simon, EFT Trainer, Internationally Renowned Psychologist featured on Denmark's DR TV series "We are Fighting to Survive", Director of Center for Emotional Focused Therapy in Copenhagen

An Emotionally Focused Workbook for Relationship Loss

Complete with exercises, reflections, and specially selected tasks, this workbook is written for those suffering from heartbreak (and their therapists) to support them in navigating and managing the pain of breakups. The authors help people in this position learn from their experiences, grow stronger from their suffering, and create healthy and fulfilling relationships.

Kathryn D. Rheem and Clare Rosoman bring their experiences as relationship therapists and devotees of attachment science to offer informed support and encouragement to the broken hearted by providing practical strategies to help readers make sense of and grow from their experiences. Mirroring the therapy process, the book is structured so that readers actively participate in their own healing process with activities that guide their journey session by session. Chapters address attachment strategies, facing fear, riding waves of anger, processing grief and loss, forgiveness, and trusting yourself again. This book will help the reader create a future in which they can know and accept themselves as the perfectly imperfect human they are and create secure bonds with the special people in their life.

This workbook is for people who have experienced the loss of a close relationship and are struggling to heal and move forward in their lives, as well as therapists assisting clients in their recovery from relationship loss.

Dr. Kathryn D. Rheem, EdD, is a couples therapist, international EFT trainer, and co-founder of the EFT Café. She has published numerous chapters including as a co-author of *Becoming an Emotionally Focused Therapist: The Workbook* 2nd edition (Routledge, 2022).

Dr. Clare Rosoman, DPsych, is a clinical psychologist in Brisbane, Australia. She is an international trainer in EFT and is the author of *An Emotionally Focused Guide to Relationship Loss: Life After Love* (Routledge, 2022).

An Emotionally Focused Workbook for Relationship Loss

Healing Heartbreak Session By Session

Kathryn D. Rheem
Clare Rosoman

Routledge
Taylor & Francis Group

NEW YORK AND LONDON

Designed cover image: Clare Rosoman

First published 2023
by Routledge
605 Third Avenue, New York, NY 10158

and by Routledge
4 Park Square, Milton Park, Abingdon, Oxon, OX14 4RN

Routledge is an imprint of the Taylor & Francis Group, an informa business

Library of Congress Cataloging-in-Publication Data
Names: Rheem, Kathryn, author. | Rosoman, Clare, author.
Title: An emotionally focused workbook for relationship loss:
healing heartbreak session by session / Kathryn Rheem, Clare Rosoman.
Description: 1 Edition. | New York, NY: Routledge, 2023. |
Includes bibliographical references and index. |
Identifiers: LCCN 2022058652 (print) | LCCN 2022058653 (ebook) |
ISBN 9781032419411 (paperback) | ISBN 9781032419428 (hardback) |
ISBN 9781003360506 (ebook)
Subjects: LCSH: Interpersonal relations. | Attachment behavior. |
Loss (Psychology) | Separation anxiety. |
Grief. Classification: LCC HM1106 .R5324 2023 (print) |
LCC HM1106 (ebook) | DDC 158.2—dc23/eng/20230227
LC record available at https://lccn.loc.gov/2022058652
LC ebook record available at https://lccn.loc.gov/2022058653

ISBN: 978-1-032-41942-8 (hbk)
ISBN: 978-1-032-41941-1 (pbk)
ISBN: 978-1-003-36050-6 (ebk)

DOI: 10.4324/9781003360506

Typeset in Stone Serif
by codeMantra

Contents

About the Authors

Kathryn D. Rheem Gratefully, Kathryn found Dr. Sue Johnson's Emotionally Focused Therapy (EFT) at the beginning of grad school after personally realizing that the only therapeutic change that lasted was change that occurred at an emotional level. Practicing and teaching EFT became Kathryn's mission and she teaches EFT internationally monthly in the EFT Café. As a certified ICEEFT trainer, she has trained clinicians in many places near and far including clinicians of US Army & Marines, US Veterans Administration, and Veteran Affairs Canada. Kathryn also writes mostly on the application of EFT with trauma and is a co-author of *Becoming an Emotionally Focused Therapist: The Workbook*. She continues to work with relationships of all orientations where good people continue to be brave session by session to restore and strengthen their bonds with those who matter most. Over the last twenty years, these good people have taught Kathryn enormous amounts by sharing their heartbreak and growing resilience. Life is hard and relationships are harder. We all suffer in life. Suffering with another, though, eases everything.

Clare Rosoman Clare is a clinical psychologist and ICEEFT-certified trainer in Emotionally Focused Therapy (EFT) from Brisbane, Australia. She is the director of the Brisbane Centre for EFT and of a psychology practice named the Brisbane Centre for Attachment and Relationships (www.attachmentbrisbane.com.au). With a wealth of experience as a psychologist, Clare has spoken nationally and internationally on EFT and is happiest when helping people to build secure connections and when inspiring other therapists in their work. Clare believes in the power of attachment and connection for all people, in all relationships, regardless of culture, structure, or identity. Clare is the author of two resource books for therapists and the self-help book named *An Emotionally Focused Guide to Relationship Loss: Life After Love*. Clare has a YouTube channel and an Instagram page to help to inspire, encourage, and support EFT therapists and those interested in attachment and relationships. Clare is continually motivated by the power of EFT, grateful to Dr. Sue Johnson for her vision, and remains committed to sharing this most amazing model of therapy with the world.

Acknowledgments

Kathryn and Clare want to acknowledge Dr. Sue Johnson for her contribution to the adult attachment literature and for her pioneering work in developing Emotionally Focused Therapy (EFT). Sue has literally changed the face of relationship therapy and has brought emotions out of the shadows and into the spotlight in the world of therapy. We are grateful to have learned from her and to have been inspired by her throughout our careers and in doing the work that we do to improve relationships.

Clare would like to acknowledge her talented co-author, Dr. Kathryn D. Rheem, for her generosity, amazing mind, and enormous heart. It was an honor to work on this special project together and to grow from her insights and perspectives. Together we have created something that we are immensely proud of. Clare would also like to acknowledge her family and especially her partner, Nicholas, for their unwavering support and belief throughout this project and in all the other harebrained schemes she comes up with. They really are an enormous source of strength and joy.

Kathryn acknowledges her remarkably talented, extremely capable, and brilliant co-author, Dr. Clare Rosoman. Clare is so gifted with her writing and artwork (she is the illustrator of all the artwork in this workbook!), so generous in her sharing, and so humbling to work with. Her humanity shines brightly and has made this project soar to great heights. So honored, Clare, to have been your partner in this amazing project! Kathryn is also so honored to have Jennifer Olden, LMFT, magnificent visionary and co-founder of the EFT Café, as a dear friend and colleague. Teaching with you, Jen, has made me a better person, honed my knowledge, and made me a better writer. And to the love of my life, Don: I love you with my whole heart.

Both co-authors would like to express deep appreciation for Heather Evans and her excellent team at Routledge. Thank you, Heather, for your belief in us. Having you in our corner has made all the difference and we thank you!

Importantly, we would like to acknowledge the collective wisdom of the special people who let us see into their hearts and share in their heartbreak and their love when they enter our therapy spaces. This workbook is an assembly of our learnings built over time, enabled by the openness and generosity of the wonderful humans we have been lucky enough to walk beside. It is our hope that the exercises in this workbook might be a vehicle to share their courage and wisdom, so that both might help others.

About our co-authorship: It is important to share that we are equal authors of this workbook. Even though one of our names must be listed first, we are proud of our shared authorship and wish there were a model and way to reflect the equal co-authors that we are. Being co-authors enriched the process immeasurably and this end product in so many ways. Working together on a foundation of trust, respect, and caring made it all possible!

Foreword

Dr. Sue Johnson

As I wrote in my 2013 book, *Love Sense: The Revolutionary New Science of Romantic Relationships,* emotion is a sharp, smart force that organizes and elevates our lives. It is what transforms existence into experience and is vital to our love relationships. The emotional highs of love expand our lives and bring our beautiful dreams into reality. But, what happens to all of this exquisite emotion when our greatest love is lost? What do we do with the pain and how do we begin to heal?

Kathryn and Clare have written the workbook to help you heal your pain. The tools you need to start navigating the emotional fall-out of losing your mate and getting your life back on track are embedded in these pages. In *An Emotionally Focused Workbook for Relationship Loss: Healing Heartbreak Session by Session,* you will feel the warm encouragement from two expert guides, you will get an overview of the science of love and what happens when that love doesn't last, and you will feel the relief of finally learning what to do with all that stubborn pain and fear.

After such a loss, give yourself the gift of starting this workbook. The authors' voices will become your companion on your darkest days – as they have for so many of their clients in therapy – and their exercises will gently walk you through your deepest aches. Science shows that walking through your aches with expert guides changes everything. As I have said before, splendid isolation is for planets, not people, and the authors have provided a lovely platform of connection session by session in this book. You will feel their support. You will get the relief that comes from facing rather than avoiding the painful echoes of heartbreak. And you will grow and heal as a result of the relatable exercises provided here.

Go on now and start your healing journey. We have all been right where you are and this workbook is a much needed resource. So glad that two of my EFT trainers, Clare and Kathryn, have brought the process of healing into focus and action within this workbook. It will be a gem for many who are reeling after loss.

Dr. Sue Johnson (EdD)
Founder of Emotionally Focused Therapy and Director
of the International Center for Excellence in Emotionally
Focused Therapy (ICEEFT)

Introduction

Let us start this book with an honest confession: I, Clare, am a hopeless romantic. I am wholeheartedly in the business of keeping relationships together. As a relationship therapist, I invest a *whole* lot into other people finding and maintaining love relationships, repairing them when they go wrong, growing together and championing each other. All in the service of the "happy-ever-after" situation. I am eternally optimistic about the resilience of humans and the power of secure connections with those who matter most to us. I am all about helping people to stay together and to find lasting love. As I said, I am indeed a hopeless romantic.

So, in creating a workbook about surviving the loss of a relationship, this is a step away from my eternally hopeful position and a step into the tough terrain of navigating loss. As an avid believer in the healing potential of secure bonds, it is easy to focus only on the building of emotional bonds. This is far easier than dealing with the devastation of the loss of those bonds. No one wants to talk about that particular thorny issue, because we all know and dread the pain that comes with this kind of loss. However, talk about it we must. I know only too well the pain of loss. That feeling that you cannot possibly endure the pain, that there is nowhere to turn and no way out of the quagmire of emotions and all-engulfing darkness. Indeed, I have loved and lost. Through relationships ending, through death, and through betrayal, I have felt like I would never survive, that I have lost my anchor and that I will drown in the sea of emotion. I have experienced the eerie silence of being left so very alone in the world; of feeling small and vulnerable and ill-equipped to manage.

I, Kathryn, write this book after enduring the kind of loss that brings many of you to these pages. My first marriage ended after my husband got his affair partner pregnant! We were supposed to be pregnant – as in, he and I. Not him and her. I never wanted to be a divorcee (like my parents!). So, I write this workbook from enduring and recovering from such a dramatic loss as I started graduate school to become a relationship therapist. Loss is so personal. It is so dramatic for each of us because it is *our* loss. *Our* pain. *Our* worst fears brought to life. After he turned away from me, I struggled mightily. I panicked. I was living scared. What would my life become? How would I carry on? What would I do next? Everything was disrupted: my home, my job, the inner-circle of my circles had exploded. Then, not six months later, my dad died unexpectedly. I was gutted, devastated, and scared. My dream vanished and fear gripped me.

Through the process of my own recovery, I realized the depth and potency of my fear, especially my unprocessed fear. I became obsessed with working with my fear because I noticed that relief would come on the other side of processing my fear. I was really angry and hurt, understandably. But I was more scared than angry or hurt and I couldn't find anybody to help me with my fear. What should I do with my fear? Positive thinking only worked temporarily. Avoiding the triggers (a common suggestion) became impossible – I would have to really narrow my life to avoid triggers. That was not practical and it certainly was not going to help me heal. I wanted to heal. I wanted to love again, someday. I needed to heal but did not know where to turn. I needed this workbook!

Between the two of us, this workbook is the culmination of a lot of enriching life experience! You just got a glimpse of some of each of our personal loss and pain and, together, we aim to have this workbook walk you through your healing process. We know the healing process firsthand and not only because we use it every day in our therapy offices. We know the healing process firsthand because we've had to heal ourselves to earn our own attachment security. Importantly, we want to walk beside you as you heal from your loss and earn your attachment security. We want this for you so that you can walk bravely into the next chapter of your life waving your resilience like a banner!

DOI: 10.4324/9781003360506-1

Working with human relationships has taught us so much about the enormity of the feelings at stake when we give our heart to another and the amazing bravery that is required to repair broken bonds. Together, we feel honored to be allowed to witness the courageous feats of love that we see before us in our therapy spaces. When people risk to open their hearts for the sake of their bond, despite considerable pain and fear, amazing things happen for them and within their relationships. We are so inspired by the wonderful humans we get to walk this path with. People are incredibly strong and resilient when their relationship really matters to them. They are capable of humility, flexibility, growth, and generosity. To see people risk, reach, and safely embrace in the dance of connection and resonance that is secure attachment is awe-inspiring. Watching distressed relationships become safe havens for love, acceptance, support, and growth is the fuel for our tanks as therapists and as human beings. When it goes well, when the road has been traveled by these people, it is as though fireworks go off, we go home at night and literally rejoice. Truly!

Each of our professional lives is all about this. You can then imagine that it is a sad time for us when people who we each genuinely care about make the life-changing decision that they just cannot stay together; that they are completely "done" and it is over. We each share in a piece of the agony when one partner's betrayal of a shared agreement shatters the trust beyond repair. We each get tied in knots when people conclude that they just do not make each other happy anymore or that they do not have it in them to keep trying. We each ache along with one partner when they are rocked with the devastating news that their special other has left them and won't return. We each share in the helplessness when one partner acknowledges that they have caused their partner pain and that they cannot windback time and take away this hurt. We see the realization appear in their eyes when they see that what has been changed cannot be changed back. It is heartbreaking when we see good people hurting like this, but sometimes this is, in fact, the sad place we find ourselves in. It is gut-wrenching. It is not what brave humans who gave their heart to another planned on when they set off on that joyous journey of falling in love.

A commitment to you...

This book is born from the darkness of the devastation of these precious bonds. It is born of hanging-out with the pain of loss, the hurt of injustice, the despair of aloneness and of wondering how you will ever feel happy ever again. It has grown from the place where you know and yearn for the wondrous feeling of love and connection and yet have experienced the desolation of its wreckage. Dear reader, our sincerest hope is that this book might offer you a hand to hold and provide you with a tiny light in those darkest moments. A tiny light that will hopefully become a strong beam to find your way out and into contact with yourself and the future you want. Our hope is that you will feel supported in your pain and that you will find growth and hope from those darkest of places. We will be there with you, as we each have with so many of the special humans we have been privileged to work with. We will help you to find some answers to these questions:

"Why does love hurt so much?"
"Will I survive this?"
"How will I ever find love again?"
"Is it me? What is wrong with me?"
"How will I ever let go?"
"How can I ever trust again?"
"What did I do to deserve this?"
"Am I choosing the wrong people?"
"How do I make sure I do not repeat past patterns?"
"How will I do it differently next time?"

These questions and many more are ones we ask ourselves when we are hurting. For many of us, we live with these questions going unanswered simply to carry on with our lives. Most do not know that these questions are answerable and, in processing and answering these questions, good people obtain peace, comfort, and clarity. This is what this book strives for: to assist you in facing these worst questions and caring for the most tender, painful places within you in order for you to find the answers that bring you peace, comfort, and clarity. We are glad you are here with us!

The physiology of relationship loss

All humans, on the verge of losing a most important relationship or as a result of losing a most cherished special someone, have a physiological reaction. Our bodies have a very clear stress response when facing such a devastating loss. Initially, simply with the threat of a rupture, break-up or separation, our bodily temperature rises and our heart rate increases. Our bodies release the stress hormones cortisol and adrenaline to get us ready to face threats and take action. With prolonged loss, it is not just our hearts that hurt and break. Along with our emotional pain, our bodily systems are impacted in real ways and we can become physically ill as we cope with relationship loss. While coming to terms with our loss, our immune system down regulates which makes it less effective in fighting off germs and infections, our cardiovascular function decreases and our hormone levels go haywire. There is a biological and physiological reality to "relationships as physiological processes"[1] and relationship loss creating pains and strains on our body and our bodily systems.

It is important for you to notice your body's responses to the stress of your lost relationship. You may find yourself feeling lethargic, eating and drinking more or less, and experiencing changes to your sleep habits and patterns. Expect some unusual physical pain that does not have another explanation. As you move through this workbook, there will be times when the exercises ask you to notice and write about your bodily sensations. They are real. We urge you to remember this as you embark on the emotional labor of processing your loss – loss has a very real impact on your physical well-being just as it does on your emotional well-being. As you continue on this healing journey, you will develop a relationship with your emotions and your body that serve you well the rest of your life!

A note on pronouns and relationship culture

You might notice throughout this book that we are sparing with the term "couple," opting to use the term "relationship" or "partnership" most of the time. While we acknowledge that many people are romantically pair-bonded and choose to enter into monogamous agreements, others do not. We want to deliberately and transparently embrace all types of relationships, whether they have two members or multiple members, whether there are expectations of exclusivity or agreements of openness. When we talk about partners or interpersonal interactions in a way that indicates only two members, that will fit for couples, but our hope is that it will also fit for the many pairs within a multi-partnered system, each pair being its own microsystem with its own special structure within the larger group. We have no expectation or assumption that the only way to prevent hurt is via monogamy. The concepts we talk about relate to any close relationship, be it romantic, platonic, or a family connection. In fact, relationship structure and definition fades into the background when it comes to matters of the heart. We are talking about something far deeper; we are talking about emotional bonds. And when a bond breaks, it hurts. We are talking about how people bond, how to survive the loss or altering of that bond, and how to forge new (and maybe stronger) bonds moving forward.

We will mix our pronouns and examples of relationships, where possible opting for gender-neutral names and using "they" as a pronoun of choice to remove gender bias and to allow the reader to hopefully connect with all examples and feel excluded by none. The examples of relationships we refer to are a collection of the many people's stories we each have encountered in our practices and all individual details have been changed to protect privacy.

This book is about relationships; all kinds of relationships and the hurt that is caused by their loss. After all, love is love and attachment bonds are bonds of the heart and it hurts like crazy when they are broken, regardless of the context.

A note to our Black and Brown readers

As white authors with tremendous unearned privilege, we are very aware that our emphasis on befriending your own vulnerability as a means for healing from loss is very different and even dangerous for our Black, Brown, Indigenous readers. As Tarana Burke[2] wrote in the anthology *You Are Your Best Thing: Vulnerability, Shame Resilience, and the Black Experience*, "My lived experience of vulnerability feels like a very dangerous place to play, an unsafe thing to even consider or think about as a Black person…Vulnerability means something very different to me" (p. xvii). Co-editor Brene Brown responded, "…the greatest casualty of trauma – including white supremacy, which is definitely a form of intergenerational systemic trauma – is that vulnerability becomes dangerous, risky, even life-threatening. But here is the painful piece – it's not like if you're Black (or Brown or Indigenous), you don't need vulnerability to experience joy, belonging, intimacy, and love. It's that we (white people) have created a culture that makes it unsafe for you to be vulnerable" (p. xviii). Within the incredible breadth and depth of Black humanity, healing takes many forms. Building a relationship with your own vulnerability and expressing your vulnerability in whatever ways work for you is our emphasis. And, as Brene's words and research highlight, vulnerability is the precursor to courage, resilience, joy, and connection. So, to our Black, Brown, Indigenous readers: find and befriend your vulnerability in the safest way, place, method you can imagine. Sometimes, vulnerability is protesting. Oftentimes, it is threaded with curse words. Sometimes it is making declarations about all that has been racist and traumatic. Other times it is about protecting your loved ones and the next generation. Sadly, what many may not see are the times you protect yourself by muting your own emotional experience to make sure the world cannot use your vulnerability against you. Whatever is needed for your safest expression of vulnerability is what we are encouraging you to seek throughout these pages.

Our friend and colleague, Dr. Paul Guillory[3], wrote *Emotionally Focused Therapy* (the type of therapy we practice) *with African American Couples: Love Heals* as a way to highlight the significance, importance, and depth of Black love. We share his wonderful book with you here with the hope that it encourages you to find your safest expression of vulnerability as you work through your loss and pain throughout these pages in order to ready yourself for your next love relationship. Love heals. Black love heals. We look forward to you feeling the healing of love again.

How to use this workbook

As we were creating the exercises in this workbook, we realized that we were more or less tracking the therapy process; as if we are with you in our therapy spaces, encouraging you to explore and reflect and to work through painful emotion. As a result, the exercises follow a sequence that we have found that many people experience in their healing journey. Feel free to work through a flurry of exercises in one go if the momentum carries you, or to make a routine out of doing a little bit each day. There are no rules on a path toward self-reflection and personal recovery from pain. How each person works through and processes their pain is as unique as they are, and no path is more "right" than another. Take your time, pay attention to how you feel after completing an exercise, and let that guide your pace. If you are left feeling churned-up and exhausted but slightly lighter, then that is a good indication that you are making great gains. Alternatively, if you are left feeling overwhelmed and fragile and teary, then that might be a sign that you need to go a bit more slowly. All speeds are OK, there is no time-limit on emotional processing and there are no prizes for being "fast."

Our aim in creating this workbook is to help you, the reader, to powerfully know your humanity – yourself as an attachment being – and to actively create change in your life that is in line with your deepest needs. This workbook is about more fully knowing and accepting yourself, making intentional changes for the better, and earning attachment security in all avenues of your life. It is about taking action and creating change in your life that will last a lifetime. This is a book about being human with us helping to guide your journey as both fellow humans and as informed professionals. So come with us. Let us take a deep dive into attachment and relationships to help you to heal and grow from this pain. We know you can do it. We will show you everything we know and give you our best.

The phenomenon and depth of emotion

There is great scientific evidence pointing to the importance of depth of emotional experiencing when it comes to healing. We have written this workbook based on this foundational knowledge as well as our own experiences of healing from great loss and pain. The ability to let ourselves feel our feelings (not simply name them cognitively) – to actually experience our feelings as sensations moving through our bodies – is the most efficient and effective method of healing. Numerous studies confirm the power of actively moving into and processing a person's moment to moment emotional experience. In referencing studies done on the therapeutic process, researchers have found that the client depth of experiencing in therapy consistently relates to positive treatment outcomes[4]. This means that the more you can lean into and feel your emotions, the more likely you are to experience healing, growth, personal insight, and positive change.

The exercises in this workbook are written with this excellent research in mind and are shaped to move you, the reader, from descriptions of external events and impersonal, behavioral descriptions of your feelings to bringing you into associating with your feelings in an experiential, self-descriptive way. Rather than writing and talking only about the events that led to your lost relationship, the exercises in this workbook will bring you closer and closer to how you are feeling about your lost relationship in order to heal and recover from your loss. The exercises will assist you in staying in contact with your feelings long enough for you to explore and elaborate on your emotional experience, which is the prerequisite to your feelings naturally synthesizing into resolution of your pain.

One goal of focusing on the depth of your emotional experience is to assist you in getting to a place where feelings and personal meanings are experienced in the moment with congruence. This means that what you are experiencing on the inside matches what you show and how you live on the outside. When we can do this, our inner world becomes a readily available resource for your thoughts and actions – like a wise guide or a compass heading. It is about the depth of emotional experience in conjunction with your ability to reflect upon and make sense of your emotional arousal. In these exercises, we want you to convey what it was or is like for you experientially in order to reconcile rather than avoid your moments of suffering and pain.

Structure of this workbook

While connected to the book, *An Emotionally Focused Guide to Relationship Loss: Life After Love,* this workbook grew from the connection between the authors, Clare and Kathryn, and a genuine desire to bring the concepts out of the therapy office and into real life for the reader. As a result of our collaboration, this workbook has its own voice and its own identity. Kathryn brings her unique style to this collaboration, blending her enormous compassion and sharp wisdom with Clare's ever-present optimism, clear and inviting writing, and perceptive reflections, earned through their years of experience as clinicians, writers, and trainers. Clare and Kathryn have pooled their over 40 years of clinical experience, learning, and leading-edge ideas in this workbook to create a practical tool for you to explore and process loss and grief and to grow stronger out of suffering.

This workbook is filled with reflective exercises and tools to create powerful moments of growth to support the reader in their healing journey. These exercises encourage personal reflection, meaning making, and identification of patterns and themes – hopefully resulting in a clearer and deeper connection with yourself. A connection with who you are, the lessons you have learned about relationships and bonding, and how you have come to navigate your closest relationships – with yourself and others. The activities and strategies introduced throughout this book provide tools for working through difficult emotional experiences, for clarifying core emotions, values and needs, and for operationalizing these in your life.

This workbook has been written as if you were sitting with one of us. We have written this workbook as if we were in a conversation with you about your pain, your fears, and your hopes. Chapter by chapter, session by session, as if in therapy with one of us, we want to walk alongside you. We hope this feels like an invitation for you to go closer to your pockets of pain in order to heal them. Unfortunately, we cannot heal our pain if we stay too far away from it. We need to go closer to it in order to work through it and to heal it. If we don't heal our pain, it blocks our options, changes our behaviors, and shrinks possibilities. **Unprocessed pain tweaks our behaviors and limits our life options. Session by session, we will help you befriend your pain in order to move through it and heal from it.**

A note to mental health clinicians and therapists

While this workbook is written directly to the person suffering from relationship loss and heartbreak, it is our sincerest hope that you will find value in working through some of these exercises with your clients in therapy sessions. We hope that you find our exercises to be relevant and illuminating for your clients as you continue to provide the good therapy you have been providing! And, we hope that the processes embedded in this workbook give your clients added support, clarity, and inspiration for their continued growth and healing.

Session One: Getting Ready to Go on this Journey

Right from the beginning, we want to honor the person you are and how you process your emotions and reactions. These exercises *must* fit with your style and who you are rather than signaling to you that you are not enough or too much. Use them in whatever way feels most meaningful to you: skip some, repeat some, modify them, use them as springboards to other reflections and awakenings. This first session focuses on what you need to help yourself go on this journey of healing with compassion for yourself, what types of activities are good self-care activities for you, and giving yourself permission to heal, to process, to feel, to get unstuck, to learn what fuels your blame, to stop avoiding. You, the reader, get to make this experience exactly what you need to heal and grow. Tell us what you are giving yourself permission to do, and we will support you!

Session Two: Love and Heartbreak

It takes a lot of courage to risk heartbreak by loving another. We know. We have risked loving and felt heartbreak too. When something important falls apart or is lost in one way or another, reflecting back on it is usually the last thing we want to do. But, when the time is right, reflecting is the only viable next step. We muster our courage to face our painful situation, as hard as that is. In this session, we will help you focus on your current or recent relationship that has left you hurt, alone, or confused. We want this session to help you to see and name the strengths of that relationship, how you contributed in positive ways, and help you find your courage to look at the painful parts. We will help you answer the question, "Why does it hurt so much?" so that you can get to know your relationship with your own vulnerability. This – your relationship with your own vulnerability – is a key factor in growth and healing. Befriending your vulnerability is the foundation to healing. We look forward to helping you do this!

Session Three: Determining Your Relationship Cycles of Distress

All relationships have cycles that include patterns of coping for each partner. Each of us copes in an individual way that contributes to our relationship dynamic or cycle. As a result, our relationship forms its own interactional cycle over time. Unfortunately, these ways of coping that we have learned to use can create emotional disconnection. Even though we love each other, our ways of coping can hurt ourselves and each other and emotional disconnection often results. Chronic emotional disconnection wears down our relationship and frays our relationship's bond. In this session, we will help you to identify the cycle that might have contributed to the tension, hurt, or dissolution of your last relationship. We do this to help you to learn from pain, and to gain valuable knowledge about where relationships go wrong. We want you to be able to take this insight forward with you into your next big love.

Session Four: Learning about Your Attachment Strategy

In this session, we share an overview of Attachment Theory while our focus is on helping you understand and name your attachment strategy. All of us have an attachment strategy that we default to in our moments of stress, worry, and aloneness. In this session, we introduce you to attachment strategies which are coping strategies that are born in our early, close relationships and come alive in all subsequent relationships. Our attachment strategies dictate how we process our emotions. As you start understanding your attachment strategy, we will also help you to name the behaviors your attachment strategy employs. Recognizing our behaviors as coping strategies due to attachment distress is the royal road to making behavioral and relational changes!

Session Five: Facing Fear

None of us like to face our fear. It is daunting, uncomfortable, and inconvenient. Most of us can easily say that there just is not enough time in the day to spend time facing our fears. Our nervous systems, though, never get a break from fear since fear is our human threat signaling system. Our nervous system is constantly evaluating our environment to ensure our safety and our survival. This is our survival imperative and it happens *below* and *behind* our awareness. We have a built-in threat-scanning system that will scan for threats to ensure our survival. This will kick in whether we think we need to be worried or afraid or not. Finding our fear, knowing our fear, allows us to access the *intelligence* embedded in our fear and all emotion, in fact. We all want to be more emotionally intelligent. Finding our fear and befriending it is the most efficient way to trust it, contain it and, ultimately, shrink it.

Session Six: Riding the Waves of Anger

Anger is the biggest emotion that humans can experience, although most of us do not understand it. In this session, we'll help you learn to ride the waves of your anger because that's what it takes to transform anger. Many try to transform their anger by denying it or by thinking "rationally" about it. If only those strategies worked! We know how uncomfortable unprocessed anger is. The body has a hard time holding it. In fact, unprocessed anger is very hard to contain, and this is why anger has such a bad rap. Its negative reputation comes from aggression that many see and associate with anger. Anger, at its essence, is a beacon for change. Once we know this, we can find the protest in our anger. Since humans do not get angry for no reason (the brain is too risk-adverse to get angry for no reason), there is always a protest that needs to be heard, validated, and respected in order for the strength of the anger to start diminishing. Anger gets repetitive when it has not been validated. In this session, we will help you find and name the protest in your anger and learn how to express your anger in safe and productive ways. There is a purity within our anger that is the beacon of change!

Session Seven: Naming and Healing Emotional Scars

Like physical injuries often leave scars and need treatment to improve, emotional injuries and trauma can leave scars which need treatment too. While it can feel extremely difficult to face our emotional scars, it is also very freeing to finally face them, speak about how we got them, and process the emotion that comes with those scars. This seems counterproductive to many people who believe it is best to leave the past in the past. The hard part about this, though, is that our bodies still hold the pain and scarring as if *still in the present*. Since emotion knows no chronology, the only way to truly move pain into the past is to process it rather than suppress and deny it. Since our survival depends on not forgetting our pain (think of a hot stove…what would life be like if we forgot the pain of touching a hot stove?), our bodies and nervous system are tasked with reminding us of our pain in order to ensure our survival. In this process of healing, naming your scars is one of the first steps in acknowledging that you have endured, and that you have suffered. We will help you to move from naming your scars, to writing about these events, and then sharing them with a safe other in order to gain the freedom that you so deserve and long for. While you might always be able to see the faint line of an old scar, after experiencing these exercises your body will actually get relief and soothing closure.

Session Eight: Processing the Enormity of Grief and Loss

We will explore what it means to confront the reality of the loss, to give up searching and fighting to recover the bond, and to plunge headlong into the despair of knowing it is forever altered and cannot be recovered. This is pretty rocky territory, but remember you are not alone, we are right here with you. In this session we dive deeply into the grief of loss. We will be naming, owning, and making room for the ruthless pain that accompanies the loss of an important relationship. We will explore and process the big, painful feelings that might be there for you, and will find what you are needing at your core to help you in your adjustment to this loss. This involves not only acknowledging the loss of someone special and all that this relationship could have been (this is extremely difficult for many), but also acknowledging the things that might have been missing for you, your unmet attachment needs (also very difficult). We will explore how you can be there for yourself and reach out to others in these most desperately harrowing moments. We will find a pathway into and through the grief and look at some strategies for riding the waves of emotion until the storm starts to pass, which although hard to believe now, it will.

Session Nine: Forgiving and Letting Go

Session Nine is where we focus on letting go. We want to help you to reconcile the pain, regret, guilt, fear, and sadness, and let go. We will help you to forgive yourself and others, where needed, and to reconcile what has happened in a way that builds your resilience. Growing from suffering does not take away the pain or mean that you have to be grateful for what has happened (far from it), but that the two states of pain and growth can and do co-exist. When we suffer, as you have, it is only natural that you would want to find meaning in that suffering. We are here to help you to find the meaning in this experience so that it can be a source of personal growth. Our wish is that this will allow you to move forwards in your life, with greater self-awareness, self-compassion, and connection with yourself. You will find that you can be healed and whole again. Your survival narrative will be a beautiful and powerful reflection of you. And we will be cheering you on every step of the way!

Session Ten: Trusting Yourself (Again)

The clearest sign of healing: you trusting yourself again. Knowing and trusting your own emotions again or, perhaps, for the first time is our shared goal in writing this workbook. It is a journey that will be so worthwhile! One very common experience of those who have lost a loved one is feeling that you lost trust of yourself while in this relationship or as a result of losing this loved one. Many people ask themselves and professionals like us, how did I lose myself and how do I get myself back? While it is common for us to hear some version of "time heals all wounds," this phrase is not actually true. If you do not spend this time healing, many people remain defensive, hurting, and mad at their losses. The simple passage of time does not heal wounds, but it can distance us from them. Temporarily, that distance from our pain can be relieving but only in a temporary way. Eventually, our pain gets bigger, takes more and more energy to suppress and ultimately does not stay inside our own skin. As you will have learned from working through this workbook, facing your pain and fears brings you back to yourself. Befriending yourself, especially your feelings, reorients you to you and your best life again and again. Trusting yourself grows implicitly as you return to your emotion!

Session Eleven: Building Security with Others

In Session Eleven, we will look at how to bring your insights about your past relationships, your attachment strategies, and your emotional awareness into your next relationship. To start this process, we will explore the beliefs and expectations you might be carrying with you, from the past, about close relationships. Then, we will help you to bravely walk back onto the playing field of romantic love with your inner security waving like a banner. We will investigate how to detect secure attachment strategies in others to ensure that you set off on the right foot. You can *now* create the relationship you want, so we will focus on *how* to shape the security that you are seeking in your new emotional bonds. We will take all you have learned about yourself and your deepest needs, and help you to honor these as you consider entering a new relationship. We will look at how to spot and avoid unhelpful dynamics in relationships, and how to earn security together as you create a loving bond with someone special.

Session Twelve: Maintaining Your Momentum

By the end of this workbook, our hope is that you will have felt supported and comforted in your loss, that you will have grown in knowledge and experience about attachment and healthy relationships,

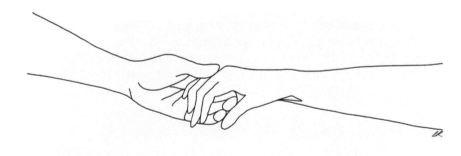

Figure 0.1 Hand to hold in the dark.

and that you will have felt into your own pain, fear, and needs in order to befriend your emotional world. In Session Twelve, we review the key take-aways from each prior session to provide you with essential reminders and some practical tools to assist you in your ongoing self-reflective work. We hope that you will take your momentum forward into a life of self-acceptance and secure bonding with your special people. That is our wish for you and for all of us; all imperfect humans finding our way in life and love. It is so much easier with a hand to hold in the dark.

Notes

1 Lewis, T., Amini, F., & Lannon, R. (2000). *A general theory of love.* Vintage Books: New York.
2 Burke, T. & Brown, B. (2022). *You are your best thing: Vulnerability, shame resilience, and the black experience an anthology.* New York: Random House.
3 Guillory, P. T. (2021). *Emotionally focused couple therapy with African American couples: Love heals.* New York: Routledge.
4 Elliott, R., Greenberg, L. S., & Lietaer, G. (2004). Research on experimental therapies. In M. J. Lambert (Ed.), *Bergin and Garfield's handbook of psychotherapy and behavior change* (5th ed., pp. 494–540). Hoboken, NJ: Wiley.

Part I

Getting Started

Getting ready to go on this journey

We know you have suffered a loss and you are hurting. And, hurting hurts, as you well know. Our aim, session by session, is to contain and decrease your pain. We are glad you are starting this journey with us. We are glad you are here. Being together with you in this process of healing is a privilege. While we feel tremendous compassion for you, we want to make sure that you have compassion for yourself as well. Treating yourself with gentleness and kindness as you work through the exercises in this workbook is extremely important.

The main task of healing from any hurt is to develop a relationship with your own vulnerability. Most of us are not taught how to befriend our hurt, pain, and other human vulnerabilities and yet knowing and sharing our vulnerabilities with safe others is the most efficient path to feeling good with ourselves, healing, and connecting with our loved ones. Our brilliant nervous systems have set up our emotions to inform us when we are vulnerable. So, getting to know your own emotional system is the most important first step to feeling better!

We invite you to begin this journey by taking a moment to reflect on the way you interact with your own emotions so that you can adjust your approach to the tools in this book in a way that will be most helpful to you. The last thing we want is for you to feel overwhelmed by the exercises that follow or for you to feel that you are somehow getting this all wrong. Right from the beginning, we want to honor the person you are and how you process your emotions and reactions. These exercises *must* fit with your style and who you are rather than signaling to you that you are not enough or too much. Use them in whatever way feels most meaningful to you, skip some, repeat some, modify them, use them as springboards to other reflections and awakenings. Then email and tell us!

Waves as a metaphor for emotions

Your emotions are yours, but they are not you. Just as waves are not the ocean. Emotions provide us humans with important information about our experiences and our needs, just as waves reflect the external and internal forces of the ocean. We are going to show you how to ride the waves of your emotions and to glean the intelligence in them throughout the exercises in this book.

Exercise 1.1

As a very first exercise, take a moment to look through these four descriptions of how you interact with your own emotions and your approach to sharing them (or not) with others. These four types of "waves" represent different emotional processing strategies that we are going to look at in detail later in this book. Don't worry if some of this feels a bit foreign now as we will take you through the typical emotional processing strategies and how they develop in later sessions. At this early stage, we are asking you to reflect on how you interact with your own emotional world. As in, do you usually try to avoid your emotions or do you tend to get swamped by them? Do you tend to share big feelings with others or keep them to yourself? This reflection marks the beginning of this important journey. Knowing more about how you greet and work with the waves of your own emotions will help us to target the exercises in this book to you personally and to assist you in making the most growth possible from this difficult time in your life.

It is normal to identify with elements of all four of the following "wave styles" or emotional processing strategies, but we encourage you to reflect on which one fits you best *in general*. Most

DOI: 10.4324/9781003360506-3

BIG WAVES - ANXIOUS ATTACHMENT STRATEGY
I experience my feelings as big waves that can knock me around.
I am very much aware of my emotional storms and I feel things very deeply.
I can feel lost at sea in my emotions and thoughts when something is
upsetting me. I can be reactive at times by blasting a big wave of emotion
in another's direction, and can then later regret my actions. Sometimes
I wish I could get a break from the intensity of the waves of my feelings.
It can be difficult to focus on practical things when I am overwhelmed by
my emotions. I really need someone in my boat with me to help me to
navigate these waves and I can feel a bit panicky on my own.

DISTANT WAVES - AVOIDANT ATTACHMENT STRATEGY
I am a little removed from the waves of my emotions. I keep things still and
calm on the surface, even though I know there might be a whole lot going
on underneath. I do not even really pay all that much attention to
my emotions, preferring to focus on practical things and my thoughts.
I like to think things through rationally and to problem-solve where I can.
I cannot really see the point in focusing on feelings that I can't solve.
I prefer to stay on the surface where it is calm and I like to row
my boat alone; it is risky to let others in, they could tip the boat.

BOTH DISTANT & BIG WAVES - HYBRID ATTACHMENT STRATEGY
In some moments, I experience my emotions as big waves which come
on strongly. I feel them deeply but I do not like the intensity. In other
moments, I experience my emotions as distant and work hard not stay
away from them. This combination – feelings coming on strongly with
intensity and, at other times, feelings being pretty far away – confuses me.
I am never really sure which strategy will help me in my worst emotional
moments. I sometimes feel jarred by the push-pull. With others, sharing
my intense feelings sometimes works and sometimes it does not and
I think that I should have kept my feelings to myself. I should have just
stayed by myself and worked to be calm again.

RIDING THE WAVES - SECURE ATTACHMENT STRATEGY
I am aware of the waves of my emotions and I stay close to them. I can
allow myself to roll with the waves if they are small and flat or if they
become more round and full. I generally can figure out what I am feeling
and I often understand why I feel a certain way. My waves tend to make
sense and I rarely feel that they are too big for me to handle or
to understand. I am OK with sitting with my feelings and riding the waves,
even the big ones, and I can give myself a break from them when they
feel too much. I am pretty good at letting others into my boat with me when
I need them, and I can reach out when I need help rowing.

Figure 1.1 Waves of emotion.

of us will notice that we default to one pattern typically. Some of us, however, will notice that our
default strategy includes a hybrid of two coping strategies: some moments we feel pretty alone in
the big waves and other moments we stay far from the waves of our emotion. This hybrid coping
strategy develops when one default coping strategy hasn't provided enough protection from the
stressors of life.

We believe that it is important to honor your way of being with your inner world throughout the
exercises in this book. For some activities, we will make suggestions for how to work with certain
exercises if your waves tend to be smaller or even hard to notice, if your waves tend to be big and a
bit overwhelming, or the combination of feeling in one moment disconnected and in the very next

moment a bit engulfed. Our wave analogy gives you an image of your inner world and a visual of how you share (or not) your distress. Throughout this workbook, you'll see how these images shift as you get to know yourself! Having an image is helpful so you can modify or adapt the strategies to work with your own style of emotional processing. Our hope is that as you learn more about attachments and relationships and your own emotional world, you can expand your ways of working with and learning from your emotions and feelings.

Finding your "wave style"

Which "wave style" do you identify most with and describe why it reflects your typical emotional expression?

_____

_____

_____

_____

_____

Like many people, you might find that more than one "wave style" fits for you. For instance, sometimes your emotional waves might feel huge and overwhelming, and other times totally flat and distant from your deeper feelings. Do you identify with two "wave styles" and if so, which two?

_____

_____

_____

_____

_____

_____

_____

Remember, all of us have emotions throughout our entire lives. Emotions are the clearest signal of being alive and yet they are often inconvenient and painful. Developing a relationship with your own emotions will texture your life and make it more colorful!

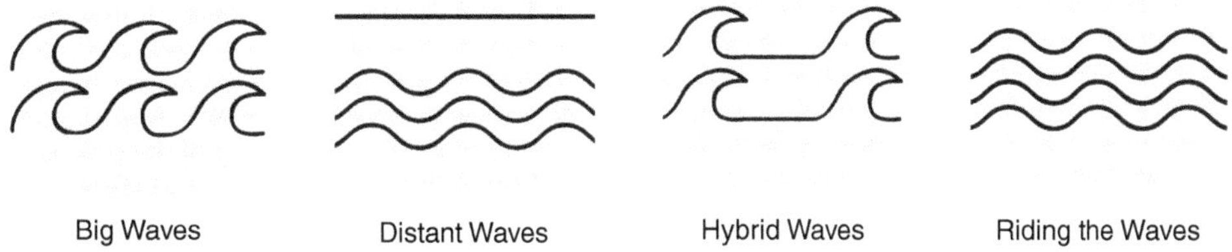

Big Waves   Distant Waves   Hybrid Waves   Riding the Waves

Figure 1.2 Circle the "wave style" that best fits you. Look out for this icon next to exercises best suited to this style of expressing and experiencing emotion.

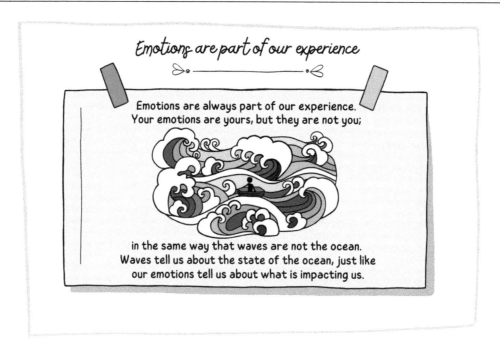

Figure 1.3 Emotions are part of our experience.

Exercise 1.2

Given your emotional processing style, the next thing we need to think about is what "pace" might be best for you when it comes to processing your emotions. For some people, they like to set a goal to do a little bit each day, others might like to set aside a block of time once a week, and still others might like to go with what feels right at any given time. As well as setting a pace that works for you, it is important to be able to take note of the impact these exercises and reflections are having on you. We encourage you to be aware of how you feel during and after an exercise so that you can become attuned to early signs that you might be feeling overwhelmed and need to "tap the brakes" or that you are emotionally stepping back from accessing your more vulnerable feelings. This might signal that you need to dive more deeply into places of pain within you. We are inviting you to reflect on how you can be gentle with yourself during this work while also noting how you can hold yourself accountable to the goals that you set and the longings of your heart. Above all, noticing your own reactions and how you feel after doing some reflective work is an excellent self-awareness skill that we aim to develop all throughout this workbook.

Given your emotional style (wave style), what might help you to make the best use of the exercises in this book? (circle)

Doing a little bit everyday	Setting aside some time once a week	Going with what feels right at the time	Pulling back if I dive too deep	Staying with it to really feel into it

What are some signs to look out for that you are getting overwhelmed and need to take care of yourself?

_____

_____

_____

_____

_____

——— What are some signs to look out for that you might be avoiding touching your more vulnerable
≈≈≈ emotions?

_____

_____

_____

_____

_____

Taking care of yourself as we start

Exercise 1.3

Processing pain and reflecting on your own experience is hard work. We commend you on your
willingness to do this. We want to reassure you that we know that this kind of emotional labor is
always worthwhile. Saying that, we also recognize how difficult it can be and how much pain it can
activate. Knowing this, we want to help you to make a plan, ahead of time, to support you as you
do this work. We are asking you to take a moment to reflect on what supports you might need, especially after emotional heavy lifting. Some things that others have found helpful after completing an
exercise are:

• Going for a walk
• Reaching out to a safe other (usually not your ex-partner)
• Being with your pets
• Being in nature
• Having a warm bath/cup of tea
• Listening to music you enjoy
• Distracting yourself with activities
• Relaxation or meditation exercises

Jot down a few ideas so that you have a support and recovery plan at the ready before we start this
work.

Things I can do to bring calm and clarity when I feel overwhelmed:

1. _____

2. _____

3. _____

4. _____

Things I can do to distract myself when I need a break from feeling too much:

1. _____

2. _____

3. _____

4. _____

Supports I can reach out to or give myself when I need them:

1. _____

2. _____

3. _____

4. _____

Anything else that I know will assist me on my journey to recovery:

1. _____

2. _____

3. _____

4. _____

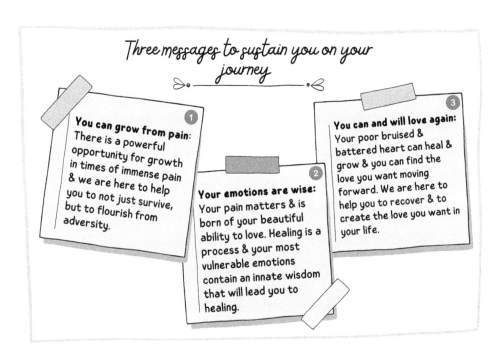

Figure 1.4 Three messages to sustain you on your journey.

Exercise 1.4

And finally, we want you to give yourself complete permission to feel *all* of your feelings. You can do this, you can grow from pain and we are right here with you. Write a personal statement of permission to yourself. What do you want to give yourself permission to do on this journey? What do you want to give yourself permission not to do? Whatever permissions you want and need to give yourself, write them out here. Writing brings clarity and adds energy to our commitments!

_____

_____

Figure 1.5 Permission slip.

Love and heartbreak

Now that you have started on this journey, let us slow down and focus on your recent relationship that left you hurting and alone. While it is hard to focus on the one that has hurt us the most, we know that we need to go closer to our pain in order to revise and heal it. We applaud your bravery in focusing on what has been the hardest for you to touch and feel. Let us start by taking stock of what is happening right now in your relationship and in your heart.

Exercise 2.1

When you think of your most recent relationship, what five words would you use to describe it?

1. _____

2. _____

3. _____

4. _____

5. _____

When you think about this relationship and write those five words characterizing it, notice what you *feel*. Write a few sentences about what you feel as you describe this most important relationship:

_____

_____

_____

_____

_____

In reflecting on your past relationship, let us look at the *strengths and challenges* of your most recent relationship.

What were the *challenges* that you faced in this relationship? For example, what hurt your heart, confused you, or left you feeling alone and uncertain?

_____

_____

_____

_____

DOI: 10.4324/9781003360506-4

Many of us have a hard time naming our positive traits, contributions, and characteristics. But here, in order to take a balanced look at your most important recent relationship, name some *strengths* that you notice. These could be strengths of the relationship, of the other person, or positive things that you brought to the connection.

_____

_____

_____

_____

_____

And now, let us have you personalize these strengths. Specifically, what did you do to contribute to the strength of this relationship? For example, you might have made a point to regularly validate your partner for their efforts. You might have shared your appreciation for your partner with them directly. You may have worked hard to slow your own reactivity.

Write out three contributions you made to your relationship's strengths:

1. _____

2. _____

3. _____

As you finish this exercise, take a few deep breaths. If you want, close your eyes so you can focus inwardly. Notice how it feels on the inside of you to name your contributions to your relationship's strengths. Can you give this feeling a name? If so, what is the name of this feeling you are having right now? _____

Imagine sharing this feeling out loud. Can you say out loud to yourself, "I feel _____ when I realize that I contributed positively to my relationship."

As you hear yourself say this statement (and it is beneficial to repeat the statement), you are feeling _____ in this moment? Simply noticing what you are feeling starts to give you some of the benefits of emotion that nature always intended for you to have!

If you felt funny or strange doing this exercise, that makes sense! Especially sharing your feelings out loud usually feels awkward. Do your best to try these new ways of healing! These are new and different ways of coping. Anything new feels strange for the first few tries. So, we appreciate you giving these new ideas your best! We so know and trust that you will feel more relief and clarity the more you try these new ways of coping.

Why does losing a relationship hurt so much?

Losing a significant love and the end of an important relationship hurts so much because your heart opens when you love another. There is no way around your heart opening when you love. In fact, it is a requirement of love. As humans, it is baked into our genetics to form close emotional bonds with others. We thrive in connection with others and in order to form bonds, we give of ourselves by opening our hearts and letting others see into our inner worlds. We are our best when we love and are loved. However, when love is lost or goes away, our heart hurts, understandably. It is excruciating. Most of us do not know what to do with our hurt. Most of us do not know what to do to heal our hurt. This workbook will teach and show you how to *be with* and to *recover from* your hurt. These exercises will bring you through a process that will address your hurt and *heal your heart*.

Most of us will feel some kind of pain when we think about an important relationship. All relationships, even great relationships, struggle. When this most important relationship is struggling or you have lost this special someone, pain is the most common experience! But, unfortunately, most of us have not had the help we have needed to learn what to do with our pain. Most of us are walking around with cracks in our hearts, pieces of our hearts broken off or parts of our hearts hardened. Nobody has taught us how to heal our pain to avoid our hearts hardening. Unprocessed pain hardens our hearts. Living with a hardened heart leaves us more defensive in life and limits our life options!

What we are offering here is a way to process your pain so that it does not limit your future options. We would like to walk with you on this journey of healing so you can benefit from our own experiences, our knowledge of the science, and our experience supporting hundreds of good people recover from pain.

As we were saying earlier, any love relationship requires that we open our hearts. That is how we *feel* love. Knowing in our heads we are loved is not enough. Love demands to be *felt*. This is how we get the benefits of love. But here is the risk: we all enter love relationships without knowing the outcome. It is risky to let ourselves love. It is risky to let love open our hearts because inevitably, our open heart is vulnerable to being hurt. And nobody sets themselves up to be hurt.

How you manage your hurt feelings

Exercise 2.2

When you think about your hurt, what do you typically *do* with it? We know, that is a strange question! But, think about it. When you are hurting, do you talk to someone about it? Do you feel it? Do you get busy to avoid it? Maybe you love feeling deeply and can even wallow in it. Maybe you have organized your life to stay far away from your hurt. Write a few sentences about what you typically do with your hurt:

_____

_____

_____

_____

_____

If you notice that you tend to become overwhelmed by the intensity of your emotional waves, can you expand on what you feel, how you experience your emotions, and what you do to manage them?

_____

_____

_____

_____

_____

_____

If you notice that you tend to stay quite distant from your emotional waves, can you expand on what you feel and how you stay distant from the pain?

_____

_____

_____

_____

_____

_____

If you notice that you can be numb to your painful feelings one minute and then drowning in them the next, can you expand on what that is like for you and how you manage in either mode?

_____

_____

_____

_____

_____

_____

Sharing the load

It turns out that science backs up and even highlights how "sharing the load" of our hurt helps to shrink it. Sharing the load with a safe other provides the co-regulation that the human brain and nervous system, especially our hearts, require.[1] It is not a choice. We are wired to cope with the stress of life with safe others. Sharing the load of our hurt and pain is not a childhood trait to outgrow. Cradle to grave, we need a few safe others to share our hurt with. When you think back over your life, who has helped you with your hurt? As a child, when you needed a band-aid, who brought one to you? After a bad day at school, who did you share with? Whose loving arms did you rely on to shelter you from the emotional storms? Who wiped your tears, cheered you up and helped you to process your pain?

Name these people here:

1. _____

2. _____

3. _____

4. _____

5. _____

If we let someone mean a lot to us and we let them into our hearts (the privileged place of being an attachment figure), the threat of the loss of this connection is destabilizing and incredibly painful. When these special connections are broken, through separation, unavailability or loss, then we will feel this loss more intensely. In fact, research shows that the pain of social exclusion activates the same parts of the brain that are active when we are physically injured. As far as the brain is concerned, social pain is equivalent to physical pain.[2] In the face of loss or unavailability of a loved one, humans fall into predictable patterns of protest and despair. This protest has been well-researched and shows clearly that we all cascade into protesting the separation and then into the despair of isolation. Some people have learned that spirited protest eventually gets them back into connection with their loved ones. Others move more quickly into detachment and withdrawing as a way to cope.

When we do not have our loved one as our secure base and safe haven, we are left alone with our emotional storms. We know that regulating our emotions on our own is very taxing and rapidly depletes our coping abilities[3]. Without the option of turning to another, we are forced to find other ways to emotionally regulate our inner worlds and to navigate the world around us. Generally, people with unavailable or inconsistent loved ones manage the distress of this in one of two ways; either by shutting their feelings down or by energetically attempting to gain contact with another. This means that some people will become adept at self-containment; pushing their feelings aside to manage the intensity and preferring to remain task-focused and practical. Others will become practiced in fighting for emotional contact by escalating their emotional signals to ensure a response from another; prioritizing the need for soothing through connection over all else.

Exercise 2.3

Think back to the loss of your most important relationship, how did you see yourself coping with the understandable overwhelming pain (circle all that apply):

I blamed. I walked away. I criticized. I cried by myself. I argued. I worked more. I traveled. I got very busy with long-overdue projects. I wallowed. I cut-off contact. I begged. I pleaded. I went silent. I got angry. I felt righteous. I avoided that person. I drank/smoked/shopped.

As you circle the ones that apply to you, notice what you are feeling. Many people feel small, alone, rejected and afraid in these worst moments of coping. What do you feel when you think about your ways of coping?

_____

_____

_____

In this quiet moment with yourself, say out loud, *"I did/do feel* _____*"* and notice what comes alive on the inside of you. Notice your body sensations and the corresponding emotion that comes alive with your body sensations. You may need to repeat your *"I feel* _____*"* three to ten times in order to feel your body sending your signals through your sensations. As you repeat your *"I feel* _____*"* statement to yourself and you notice your body's sensation come alive, add some movement like walking, singing, deep breathing. Since emotions form the bedrock of our sensations[4] and live in our bodies, movement facilitates the body's release of emotions.

About vulnerability

One of the keys to healing from relationship loss is to befriend our own vulnerability. All of us feel vulnerable throughout life. This fact bears repeating: *all humans feel vulnerable regularly.* It is a fact of being human and alive. Most of us, however, do not want to feel vulnerable and, as a result, do not pay attention to our vulnerability. What we mean here is that we can easily ignore or avoid our softer, tender emotional worlds where our vulnerabilities lie. This part of our experience is rich in meaning and wisdom! We each need to befriend our vulnerability in order to grow ourselves emotionally as we age and to increase our life's options (since not knowing or befriending our vulnerability decreases our life's options). We all do things to avoid our vulnerability; we often have a range of ways we avoid this place that lives inside us. It is especially difficult to feel vulnerable as a result of losing a loved one. There is no more vulnerable time in life than the time after an important relationship ends or is lost. In order to fully heal, we all need to face our own vulnerabilities. We need to increase our comfort in feeling vulnerable. We need to befriend and have a day-to-day relationship with our vulnerability, which takes courage and strength. **Are you strong enough to be vulnerable?**

Exercise 2.4

How do you feel about your own vulnerability?

_____

_____

_____

When you remember feeling vulnerable, what memory emerges?

_____

_____

_____

When you are vulnerable, do you ever let anyone know you feel vulnerable? If so, to whom do you turn?

_____

_____

_____

What do you usually do with your vulnerability? Do you deny it? Dismiss it? Talk about it? Feel it?

_____

_____

_____

While feeling vulnerable is uncomfortable, it is what makes us human. None of us look forward to being or feeling vulnerable. It is uncomfortable to feel vulnerable. Making friends with our vulnerability is a hallmark of emotional maturity, although we are sure nobody has ever told you that! The main point of making friends with our vulnerability is so that our vulnerability and the intelligence that comes from it guides us throughout our lives. We all make zillions of decisions every day and the big decisions we make must be aligned with our hopes, dreams, and goals. Befriending our vulnerability is one key way of orienting ourselves decision-by-decision to make sure we are congruent with our minds and hearts! Therefore, living the life we were meant to live.

Ideally, our loved ones will know their own vulnerability at least a little bit. A relationship where each partner knows a bit of their own vulnerability is a relationship that will be emotionally attuned and responsive, two essential components of any love relationship that has attachment security. In order to be an attuned and responsive partner, we need to reference our own vulnerability within ourselves as a foundation of the empathy we offer our loved ones in their moments of need.

As we end this second session, we want you to know how proud we are of you! Love and heartbreak is so painful and so hard to heal. But when we yearn to heal, especially to love again, befriending our vulnerability is vital in order to heal our hearts and grow from our loss. Going closer to our humanity – our vulnerabilities – takes all kinds of strength. Sometimes, our loved ones and our societies do not recognize these strengths as true, core strengths. This is a paradigm shift that we all need to make: **feeling our feelings and befriending our vulnerabilities are core strengths even if not recognized as traditionally strong.** So, acknowledge your courage to feel, your bravery in working with your vulnerabilities (that all humans have!), and your strength to continue your healing. We are so glad to be here with you!

Figure 2.1 On love and vulnerability.

Notes

1 Coan, J. A. & Sbarra, D. A. (2015). Social baseline theory: The social regulation of risk and effort. *Current Opinion in Psychology, 1,* 87–89.
2 Eisenberger, N. I., Lieberman, M. D. & Williams, K. D. (2003). Does rejection hurt? An fMRI study of social exclusion. *Science, 302,* 290–292.
3 Coan, J. A. & Sbarra, D. A. (2015). Social baseline theory: The social regulation of risk and effort. *Current Opinion in Psychology, 1,* 87–89.
4 Levine, P. (2015). Presentation at the *Psychotherapy Networker Symposium.* Washington, D.C.

Determining your relationship cycle of distress

All relationships have cycles that include patterns of coping for each partner. In our cases, we are experts in Attachment Theory and Emotionally Focused Therapy (EFT)[1], [2] which helps us see, understand, and interrupt each partner's pattern of coping through the lens of attachment. These coping strategies are called attachment strategies. Typically, each person has a default attachment strategy which is a set of behaviors used to protest the distance or closeness in an important relationship. Escalations in relationships are fueled by each partner's attachment strategy being activated.

Common relationship cycles

A very common relationship escalation cycle is when one partner copes by turning up the emotional heat and the other partner tries to turn down the emotional heat. Neither coping strategy is better or worse, and each serves an incredibly important function from an attachment perspective. One turns up the emotional heat to get reassurance that they matter and that the other will respond to them. One turns down or tries to turn off the emotional intensity because it is overwhelming and leaves them feeling like they never measure up. Each strategy functions to keep the partner from getting too close or too far away.

Understandably, each partner wants more or less closeness. In our moments of need or suffering, some of us want a lot of closeness, comfort, and contact. Others of us want space, alone time, and quiet. As a relationship grows, together we develop relationship patterns of coping. Each of us copes in an individual way that works well for us individually, but how we cope impacts our loved one just as their way of coping impacts us. This is how relationships form their own cycles over time. The cycle that develops usually works well until facing a life-stressor or being caught in an era of multiple stressors. When facing an overwhelming stressor or era of stress, the relationship's coping pattern starts to escalate which typically pushes each partner to cope individually. Individual coping leads to relationship disconnection. Since emotion is the messenger of love[3], emotional disconnection is the largest threat to any love relationship.

Once we get emotionally disconnected from our loved one, we default to our individual coping strategies. Embedded in these individual strategies are habitual ways of making meaning. Typically, we tend to make meaning about ourselves and our loved one (we call these thoughts "attributions"). For example, a common attribution is that "I am inadequate" or "they are impossible to please." Attributions are our interpretations or theories that allow us to make meaning about characteristics that we judge to be negative. They can play a role in emotional disconnection and make us more stubbornly hold our position or close us off from hearing the other or seeing another perspective. Our attributions are usually not all that accurate but tend to be informed by our experiences in close relationships and with our particular partner.

Exercise 3.1

In thinking about the loss of your recent love relationship, what attributions did I make about myself when we were emotionally disconnected?

DOI: 10.4324/9781003360506-5

What attributions did I make about my partner?

_____

_____

_____

_____

What did I say about myself to myself? For example, "this is too much" or "I am over this."

_____

_____

_____

_____

It is these attributions – fueled by pain and suffering – that usually do not allow space for our own or our partner's vulnerabilities to be known, seen or felt. These attributions become self-perpetuating as each partner becomes more defensive and reactive. As we continually react, we need our defenses more and more. The more we need and use our defenses, the further away we get from our vulnerabilities, softer feelings, and fears. Our softer feelings, vulnerabilities and fears are the very details that need to be shared to create emotional connection. As we get more and more defensive, the less we share and the more emotionally disconnected we become and remain.

The role of coping strategies in relationship cycles

EFT research has shown that partners get stuck in repetitive escalations or relational cycles where the way they each signal what they need is experienced by the other as negative. We all do what feels most obvious to us when we are distressed about our most important relationships. Unfortunately, the way one person signals their need can feel threatening or discombobulating to the other. For instance, it might make sense for one partner to get louder when they sense the other's distance, or one might become quieter and pull away when they sense tension from or with the other. This way of signaling a threat to the connection can unwittingly become a trigger of alarm for the other. One partner getting verbally louder might be experienced as threatening for the other or one partner's silent retreat might be experienced by the other as abandoning. When under threat, it is normal for people to react in their best way in order to manage their emotional disequilibrium. These reactions are coping strategies that allow us to maintain our emotional balance, even if it does not help our relationship's connection at the moment. Inevitably, these coping strategies are experienced as alarming for the partner and can even confirm their attributions of the other as not caring/being scary/wanting to fight/being impossible to please.

Exercise 3.2

Here are some examples of how partners might turn up the emotional heat to seek closeness (trying to register on the other's radar):

- Demanding and complaining
- Being critical
- Expressing emotions in loud, amplified ways
- Following the other around in order to get their attention

 These strategies are most associated with a wave style of "big waves" of intense emotion that urgently needs to be soothed by another's responsiveness and reassurance.

Here are some examples of how partners might turn down the emotional heat to seek distance (trying to prevent conflict):

- Withdrawing or going silent
- Focusing on other things
- Problem-solving or analyzing
- Avoiding being around the other

———
≈≈≈≈ These strategies are most associated with a wave style of "distant waves" where someone stays away from the emotional intensity by pulling away from contact.

Sometimes people use a mixture of these two coping strategies: turning up the heat and turning down the heat. This often represents a longing to be close but a fear of being hurt that can mean you send confusing push-pull signals to others.

Most often people will predominantly use one of these attachment strategies, but if you use both, you can note this below. What is your coping strategy (when you feel disconnected from your partner)?

_____

_____

_____

_____

When you are using your coping strategy, what behaviors are you doing?

_____

_____

_____

_____

What emotions are you feeling?

_____

_____

_____

_____

What did your partner do in response to your behaviors?

_____

_____

_____

_____

Then, what would you do?

_____

_____

_____

_____

The role of signals in relationship cycles

In your recent relationship's cycle of distress, the next element to highlight and understand is how you each sent signals of distress to one another. How we each signal our needs to our loved ones can make or break whether our needs get met! And, when we are off-balance, none of us send a "soft" signal of distress! It is very common for one partner to signal a need in the heat of the moment that the other partner experiences as triggering. Once triggered, any responsiveness they might have had is blocked and it is much harder to respond in caring ways.

Exercise 3.3

What signals did you send of your needs to your partner?

_____

_____

_____

_____

How did you let your partner know that you were struggling, in need?

_____

_____

_____

_____

An example

Let's look at an example of a common cycle of distress between partners. The cycle of distress between Sam and Jordan (an inter-racial, cisgender, queer, monogamous, same-sex couple married for 27 years) recently escalated after their youngest child left for college. When it was just the two of them at home together, it felt surprisingly awkward, a bit off-balance, and more than a little distant. Sam started working longer hours at work and Jordan started complaining more about Sam's longer hours. In earlier times together, they would often talk longingly about their free time together when all the kids would finally be away at university! Well, when that time finally arrived, it did not feel good or in any way like they imagined all those years ago.

At least one or two days a week, Jordan promised himself he would not complain but when Sam finally got home, his complaints came spilling out. As Sam heard the tone of Jordan's complaints, his body stiffened and he exhaled. He had worked a long day, a long week in fact. But, he did not appreciate it and was now complaining again about it. As he exhaled, he did not know what to say. He could not imagine sharing any kind of vulnerability and instead became defensive. He said, "I'm doing the best I can. You should be grateful that I make a good salary." Jordan felt the sting of his defense, but could not imagine sharing anything vulnerable. Jordan also became defensive as he reacted to Sam's statements. Jordan said, "Work is so much more important to you than I am, Sam." He said, "Oh, you think I like to work these long hours?" Jordan reacted with, "Well, you must, since you do it all the time!"

Of course, each of them was hurting on the inside and each of them had needs that they were not signaling. Jordan thought Sam did not care about his experience or his needs. Sam thought that Jordan would never be happy with him and Jordan could never be satisfied. These attributions they each made escalated their cycle of distress again and again which left them each feeling lonely and scared. Notice how neither Sam nor Jordan really shared any vulnerability with the other? Neither said, "I miss you," or "I'm sorry I complained," or "Sorry I was at work so late." The signals they sent each other were the scrambled signals of distress and defenses all mixed together. Each reacted with their individual coping strategy that usually has the effect of pushing our loved one further and further away.

The consequences of a negative cycle

The problem with this common cycle is not just that the signals of need get scrambled and missed, it is that the consequence of experiencing your partner as triggering and emotionally unavailable or unsupportive erodes or even destroys the emotional connection you both want and need so much! Remember, it is the emotional connection that suffers most when partners default to their individual coping strategies.

Except in a relationship where one or both partners use coercive control, we each contribute to our relationship's cycle of distress. For more information about coercive control, see *An Emotionally Focused Guide to Relationship Loss: Life After Love* (page 19)[4]. We write this knowing that we too have hurt our loved ones in moments and we have missed opportunities to be there for our partners, just as they have missed our moments of need. Many of us get critical of our partners just when we need them the most. Usually, these criticisms push our partners further away, although we are longing for them to come closer! Others of us get quiet and distant thinking that distance will settle each partner's emotions. Our good intent tells us to take space but that often leaves our partners feeling alone and unloved. Sometimes we cope by engaging in painful behaviors like yelling and screaming or saying mean things. Sometimes our silence leaves our person feeling abandoned by us right when they need us. It is in these moments that our best attempts to cope when we are triggered can damage our most precious bonds. This is not because it is our intent, but because coping strategies are inherently isolating; they help the individual in the moment, but work against the creation of a safe and secure bond in the long term.

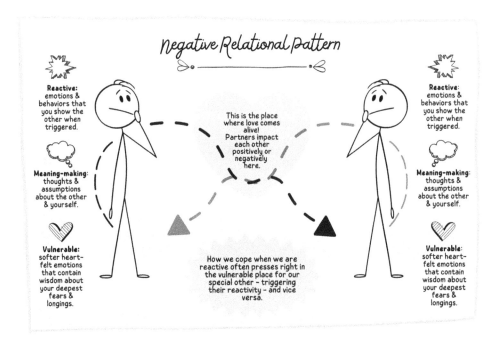

Figure 3.1 Negative relational pattern illustrates the elements of a negative relational pattern between partners.

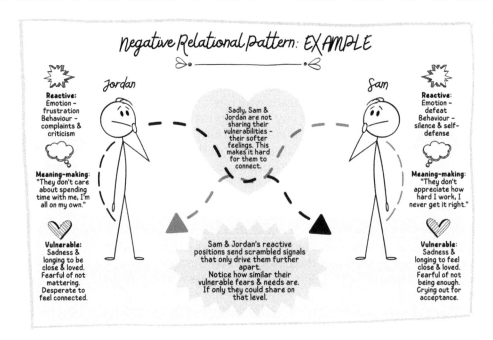

Figure 3.2 Negative relational pattern, you will see the example of Jordan and Sam's negative relational pattern. Notice how they each sent reactive signals that blocked closeness?

Vulnerability as the antidote

In these next exercises, we are asking you to be vulnerable with yourself as you answer these questions. Being vulnerable with yourself includes being gentle and compassionate with yourself as you name actions and impacts that don't feel good to you. We will discuss this more in future sessions, but we want to offer a new frame on vulnerability: it is a new strength to be vulnerable.

Exercise 3.4

In your recent relationship, what did you do that you do not feel good about?

_____

_____

_____

_____

_____

What did your partner do that you did not like?

_____

_____

_____

_____

_____

These ways of coping that we do not feel good about usually create emotional disconnection. Even though we love each other, our ways of coping can hurt ourselves and each other and emotional disconnection results. Chronic emotional disconnections wear down our relationship and fray our relationship's bond. Research into relationship distress tells us that the most common problem that relationships face is emotional disconnection.[5] While it may seem that conflict is what is causing the trouble, often it is the emotional distance – not the conflict – that best predicts whether a relationship will flourish or disintegrate. It is normal for partners to have disagreements and upsets, but so long as they can emotionally reconnect, they can nurture their bond and repair any ruptures. Ruptures are breaks in the attachment connection between people who love each other. Ruptures happen when the other seems to be unavailable, non-responsive or regularly dismissive. When signals of need are not communicated clearly, it is little wonder that emotional disconnection is the result.

Exercise 3.5

Now that you know more about relationship distress cycles and what drives them, think about what you were desperately missing in your recent and/or most important relationship.

Step back from all the messy details of what went wrong and why, or the ins and outs of the complicated topics you disagreed about and reflect on what you were really crying out for from your partner at a deep heart-level that they missed.

Write that here:

_____

_____

_____

_____

_____

_____

While you might have become critical of your partner or shut them out to prevent more conflict or had given up trying to be heard, ask yourself what you were really longing for in those stuck moments. Write that longing out here:

_____

_____

_____

_____

_____

_____

What were you most starving for that you really needed in this relationship?

_____

_____

_____

_____

If you wanted something in particular (like more sex, to agree on parenting, more time together, less spending and more saving, a new house), ask yourself, "If I got that, what would that tell me about the relationship?"

_____

_____

_____

_____

What does it tell me about my partner?

_____

_____

_____

About myself?

_____

_____

_____

What need in me would be soothed?

_____

_____

_____

_____

What worst fear in me would be quieted?

_____

_____

Suspend that part of your brain that wants to use reason and logic here and instead, try to connect with the deeper, more emotional parts of you that were crying out for something soft and caring from your partner. We are digging for your attachment needs here. Close your eyes and really let yourself feel into the core of your distress...write your deepest needs and longings here:

_____

_____

_____

_____

Figure 3.3 A few things to remember.

What is it like for you to feel that longing now? What do you feel in your body? What feelings show up? This is an important step in tuning into yourself – your own emotional world and listening to your inner wisdom!

As we start to wrap up Session Three, notice what you are feeling inside yourself. Take a few deep breaths. You have done a lot of important work here and all of this is very evocative. It is hard work to focus on our coping strategies and how our coping strategies played out with our partner and interacted with their coping strategies. Remember to be gracious and compassionate with yourself. Good people get caught in distressing relationship patterns all the time. The important part is that you are learning about your coping strategy now as you get to know yourself!

Notes

1   Greenberg, L. S. & Johnson, S. M. (1988). *Emotionally Focused Therapy for Couples*. New York: Guildford Press.
2   Johnson, S. M. (2020). *The Practice of Emotionally Focused Couples Therapy: Creating Connection* Third Edition. New York: Routledge. (First ed. 1996).
3   Lewis, T., Amini, F. & Lannon, R. (2000). *The General Theory of Love*. New York: Vintage Books.
4   Rosoman, C. (2022). *An Emotionally Focused Guide to Relationship Loss: Life After Love*. New York: Routledge.
5   Gottman, J. M. (1994). *What Predicts Divorce? The Relationship Between Marital Processes and Marital Outcomes*. Hillsdale, NJ: Lawrence Erlbaum Associates, 1994 print.

Learning about your attachment strategy

In this session, our focus is on helping you understand and name your attachment strategy. Attachment strategies are coping strategies that are born in our early, close relationships and come alive in all subsequent relationships. All of us have an attachment strategy that we default to in our moments of stress, worry, and aloneness. As you start understanding your attachment strategy, we will also help you to name the behaviors your attachment strategy employs. Recognizing our behaviors as coping strategies due to attachment distress is the Royal Road to making behavioral and relational changes!

In Session Three, we focused on your coping strategy and how it came alive and played out in your relationship. In this chapter, Session Four, we will take a deeper dive into how your coping strategies came to be and learn how to track your strategy and ultimately interrupt it.

Attachment theory

Attachment theory has a lot to teach us about our human need for close and loving relationships. For much of the 20th century, we believed that children should grow up to be independent and that self-reliance was a goal of mature adulthood. Many people still firmly believe this, but thanks to the revelations of John Bowlby's attachment theory[1] and an army of subsequent researchers examining child and adult attachment, we now know that forming loving bonds with responsive others is vital to our wellbeing as humans throughout our whole lives. It is clear that everyone has an innate yearning for trust and security with one or a few irreplaceable others. Bowlby believed that we need others in this way "from the cradle to the grave."[2] We do not grow out of our attachment needs. Far from being dysfunctional, relying on special others allows a person to flourish and to take what life has to offer, safe in the knowledge that they have someone to turn to when things get hairy.

For some people, acknowledging our need for others as we navigate life might feel like a no-brainer, as obvious as our need for oxygen. However, for other people the idea that we are built to connect with others and to rely on them in times of need might feel really foreign or even threatening. This reaction is usually grounded in the experiences you have had with close relationships with important people throughout your life.

Our early attachment relationships teach us important lessons about what it means to be close to another, whether others can be a resource or not, and whether we are worthy of love and support in times of need. Our earliest attachment figures' sensitivity and responsiveness to our needs is crucial in developing our sense of security in the world and confidence that others will also be responsive to our needs. This security and trust in others then transfers into feeling more confident in yourself to navigate challenges. These formative relationships set our expectations for our subsequent relationships, like a blueprint in a way, and impact our belief in our own ability to face life's challenges.

Bowlby was adamant that it is not immature or pathological to turn to another person in this way, believing that this was in fact a biological imperative with adaptive value.[3] Building on Bowlby's ideas, attachment scientists have shown us that the bond that adults form with romantic partners mirrors the bond a child forms with their attachment figures[4]. Our attachment figures as adults serve the very same functions as our primary caregivers did in childhood. In this way, we can conceptualize romantic love as an attachment bond. Partners can offer the same safe haven of support to turn to and a secure base for venturing out into the world, as a parent offers a child. It is so natural to want to turn to your special other (or others) when you need comfort, that we actually never outgrow this need. We gain strength from the knowledge that we have someone watching our back and can then more bravely

DOI: 10.4324/9781003360506-6

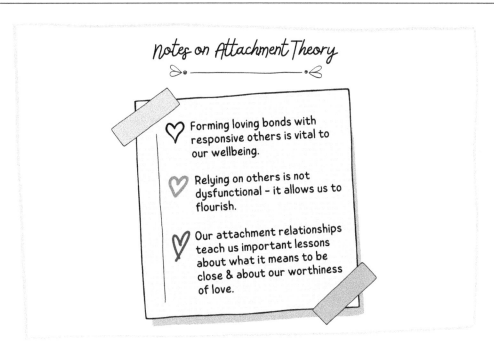

Figure 4.1 Notes on attachment theory.

engage with the world around us. With this knowledge, we can be curious, can take calculated risks, and can put our best foot forward.

Exercise 4.1

Growing up, think about your closest relationships with your key attachment figures (these are the people you named in Session 2).

What did they do that felt comforting and soothing for you?

_____

_____

_____

_____

_____

How did they reassure you when you felt uncertain? How did they give you courage to try again, to believe in yourself, or to learn from a mistake? How did they offer this?

_____

_____

_____

_____

_____

Could you rely on them to be there when you needed them? How did you know this?

_____

_____

_____

_____

_____

How did it feel to take your joys or worries to them? Did it make you feel a bit better or worse? What meaning did you make about this?

_____

_____

_____

_____

_____

Were there people in your world who could have been attachment figures but were unavailable, distracted or frightening in some way? If so, how did this impact you? What did you do with your sad/scared/hurt feelings?

_____

_____

_____

_____

_____

If you did not have safe and available caregivers as attachment figures in your life growing up, take some moments to let yourself feel the sadness around this. This is very hard on a little person's heart and that heartache does not go away on its own. Please give yourself loads of compassion in this moment for all the times of uncertainty or distress where your need to have a safe other to turn to went unmet.

If there wasn't someone to turn to, how did you manage when you felt scared, sad, unwell or discouraged?

_____

_____

_____

_____

_____

_____

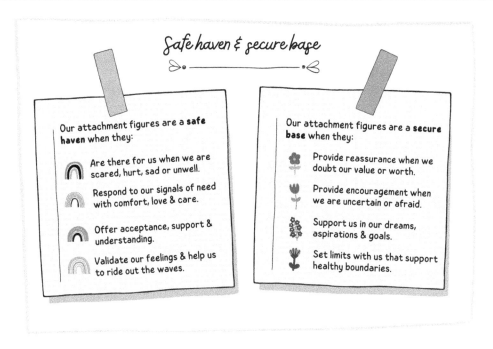

Figure 4.2 Safe haven and secure base.

Safe haven and secure base

Attachment theory has crystalized our understanding of our need for a "safe haven" and a "secure base" as humans. Our attachment figures perform these two really important functions, and they might look different in different cultures and different family structures. Essentially, attachment figures provide *comfort,* and they provide *reassurance.* We all need someone safe to turn to when we feel uncertain, and we need encouragement to take on challenges. These are two sides of the attachment coin that help us to develop into fully functional humans, ready to live life to the fullest. If we can turn to a "stronger, wiser other" when threatened, frightened, vulnerable, sick, or uncertain, then they are a haven for comfort and protection – their loving care helps us to soothe and regulate our emotions. Their support and reassurance that we are loved and safe then becomes a strong and stable platform underneath our feet to venture out from. This starts in childhood, in our earliest attachment relationships and we need it for our whole lives.

Secure attachment bonds

We all know that if our special person is there when we need them and responds to our vulnerability by showing interest and care, we feel better, and "doing" life is just that little bit easier. This is the result of our attachment figures responding to our signals, showing that they care about us and demonstrating that they are here for us. These are the most important elements of a gold-star-worthy attachment figure; they are accessible, responsive and engaged. Dr. Sue Johnson, the founder of Emotionally Focused Therapy calls this the "A-R-E" of secure attachment[5]. When we are responded to in this way, we learn to regulate our emotional storms, that connection is a good idea, and that we are worthy of love and comfort. This does something very powerful to our inner-worlds: it directly impacts how we see ourselves, others, and the world around us. We internalize this ability to self-soothe from being soothed by responsive attachment figures. We begin to feel competent in managing our emotional highs and lows and we develop a sense of confidence that others are dependable and reliable. Paradoxically, when we know we have people to turn to, we then do not need them as much. This is what we call "secure attachment."

When attachment is working beautifully, there is a lovely balance between seeking closeness and tolerating distance; there is a flexibility in the bond between people who matter to each other.

When we know that our few very special and irreplaceable others are there to turn to in life's shaky moments, then we can be brave. The security that these connections offer us is invaluable. This does not mean that we are weak or dependent on our partners. This is what Bowlby called "functional dependence" or what we can think of as effective dependency[6]. In relationship, we grow. The more securely we can feel our important other's responsiveness, the more autonomous and confident we can be.

Attachment strategies

An attachment strategy is the term used to describe a person's way of navigating their attachment relationships and their emotions when they are under threat. Stemming from our experiences with and expectations of others, an attachment strategy is our way of *signaling our needs* and our way of *managing our own emotional world*[7]. An attachment strategy describes how a person tends to manage when their attachment system fires up into action. When we perceive that our needs for contact and comfort from our special other are in jeopardy, we are thrown off-balance emotionally.

Exercise 4.2

Notice for a minute how you tend to cope with attachment-related pain. Think back to the exercises in the last session where we reflected on how you showed up in your last relationship – how you signaled your distress (or not).

- Do you tend to keep it to yourself, to put it away and to busy yourself with other things to manage the enormity of touching it?
- Or do you feel it intensely and make repeated attempts to turn to others for soothing only to find that elusive?
- Or do you at first reach out to another for reassurance or contact, only to become scared of the possibility of being hurt, so then pull away and cope alone (or vice versa)?

As a child, how did you let your attachment figures know when you needed them? Did you get bigger or louder to get on their radar, or did you pull away, preferring to cope alone? Or did you do a mixture of both those strategies? Write what you did here:

_____

_____

_____

_____

_____

You might notice similarities or differences in how you signaled your attachment needs (for comfort or reassurance) in your earliest attachment relationships and your adult relationships.

What is similar? E.g. I still amplify my signals but instead of crying like I did as a child I now can "nag" my partner to get them to hear me – this is still me insisting the other responds to me.

_____

_____

_____

What is different? E.g. Instead of pulling away and coping alone, I now get really upset and angry if my partner is not available to me – I never want to feel alone like that again.

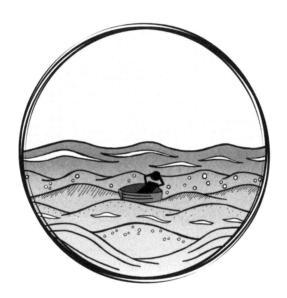

Figure 4.3 Secure attachment strategy.

Secure attachment strategy

When a person exhibits the flexibility of reaching out to a safe other for comfort and reassurance and can also travel bravely out into the world, we describe them as having a "secure attachment strategy." Someone with a secure attachment strategy is likely to both be autonomous and able to seek and take in care from another. They can clearly signal their need as required and can confidently go out into the world. They are comfortable with closeness and with distance and can flexibly move between the two. This is what we are wired for and if we have this flexibility and capacity, we thrive, but if we do not have it, we have a steeper hill to climb. Examples of secure attachment strategies are: being able to let another know when you need help or comfort, being able to offer help or comfort to another without becoming overwhelmed, being able to clearly signal your needs in ways that do not trigger the other, being able to ride out inner-emotional storms without becoming overly dysregulated, trusting in one's own ability to manage challenges, being able to call a special other to mind to sustain you in a wobbly moment, and knowing that others are there if you need them.

Figure 4.4 Anxious attachment strategy.

Anxious attachment strategy

People with an anxious attachment strategy have learned that their attachment figures are likely to be unreliably available and they manage this by energetically pursuing connection with their special person to make sure that they will be available to them. They learned (for good reason) that they need to turn up the heat on their emotional signals, in order to get on their attachment figure's radar. Bowlby called this "attachment protest" which is a perfect way of describing the intent behind anxious, pursuit behaviors. People who have an anxious attachment strategy live with a high amount of *fear* that their special person will not be there for them and will reject them. As a result, they are often very alert to perceived threats to their bond.

Examples of an anxious attachment strategy include protesting perceived distance, increasing the intensity of the plea for connection through raising your voice or using more evocative language, clinging, escalating demands, or becoming critical. This can also include scanning for possible threats to the relationship (born of worry about possible abandonment), seeking reassurance that you are loved, and throwing lots of energy at the problem of the disconnection. Because an anxious attachment strategy involves turning up the emotional heat, you can be perceived by others as overwhelming, confrontational, irrational, or intimidating. This attachment strategy is driven by fear of the loss of connection. As a result, the special other's lack of response is unbearable. People who use an anxious attachment strategy see *connection* as the solution to their emotional uncertainty and aim to desperately seek it to soothe their jangling attachment alarms.

Figure 4.5 Avoidant attachment strategy.

Avoidant attachment strategy

An avoidant attachment strategy aims to help a person to turn down the heat on their emotional signals. People who tend to use an avoidant attachment strategy have learned that their attachment figures are unavailable and dismissing of their needs for comfort and reassurance. As a result, they have come to the sad conclusion, often very early in life, that it is not a good idea to take their attachment needs to another – that it does not make things better. Instead, they learn to manage the storms of their emotions by suppressing and not taking them to another for soothing. Without the help of co-regulation with a safe other, they are left to cope alone. This is no easy task, and this is where an avoidant attachment strategy helps a person to cope when safe co-regulation with another is not an option. Being left alone, coping alone, is not an easy feat for any human, and to do this, they have to suppress their need for others (fight their biology), squash their emotional pain and stay very practical and logical to manage all by themselves. In fact, in order to suppress emotional intensity, a person may utilize drugs, alcohol, or other substances to avoid their emotions. Bowlby called this "compulsive self-reliance" and sadly, this is an image that is still held up in some societies (particularly Western) as healthy, high-functioning, and mature.

An avoidant attachment strategy can include: moving away from your own or your special other's emotions (sometimes appearing dismissive or unfeeling), retreating to regulate alone, preferring to stay very logical and problem-focused, going into self-defense, or trying to avoid conflict. Because an avoidant attachment strategy means that you self-regulate, you may come across to others as cold or distant. The function of an avoidant attachment strategy is to signal your need for harmony by trying to protect the relationship from the damaging impact of conflict. These strategies stem from the conclusion that distance is the best solution to the threat to the bond and aim to "put out the fire."

Figure 4.6 Hybrid attachment strategy.

Hybrid attachment strategy

Some people use a hybrid of both anxious and avoidant attachment strategies (ways of coping). We describe this combination as a *"fearful-avoidant" attachment strategy.* This stems from fear about the reliability of the other's responsiveness and avoidance of closeness to protect against hurt and rejection[8]. This means that a person may anxiously pursue their loved one for contact, but then feel frightened by the risk of hurt in becoming so emotionally close, that they then pull back to avoid emotional intimacy. A hybrid attachment strategy is associated with having had frightening, erratic, or abusive early caregivers who were inconsistent, unpredictable, and unsafe. To have to rely on caregivers like this puts a child in an untenable position where their very natural attachment needs drive them to seek connection with caregivers who do not offer them a secure base or safe haven. This is completely destabilizing for a child and severely impacts their trust in others. It is then an act of supreme bravery and endurance for people with this early experience of relationships to even consider opening their heart to another as adults. Despite emotional connection being so painful, people who use a hybrid attachment strategy show amazing endurance when they still seek love and closeness, but can become terrified of allowing another in. They can become extremely fearful of hurt, betrayal, or loss, and can become emotionally dysregulated in the face of such an enormous risk. As a result, a hybrid attachment strategy can involve the sending of confusing signals to attachment figures such as energetically pursuing for connection, rapidly followed by panic with this closeness, and then retreat and shutdown to avoid vulnerability and potential hurt. A sort of rapidly cycling push-pull "I want you…I don't want you." This can confuse or even push away well-intentioned partners who long to provide the healing experience of a safe, loving connection. Above all else, a fearful-avoidant attachment strategy is about a need for safety in close relationships.

Attachment strategies are coping strategies

Attachment strategies are the things that we do when turning to another for co-regulation is not an option. The state you find yourself in and what you do when triggered like this, is actually your best attempt to regain emotional equilibrium in the absence of being able to use the most efficient channel of regulation, which is turning to a safe other. For that reason, attachment strategies are *adaptive*. We see attachment strategies as coping strategies or protective strategies. Coping strategies perform two important functions:

1. They help us to manage our emotions in the moment and,
2. They aim to protect us from more attachment-related hurt.

In this way, our attachment strategies are *adaptive coping strategies* that have been learned in relationships. They are learned in your earliest relationships and become a tool to reach for when your attachment alarms go off in your subsequent relationships. While they protect you from hurt or help you to manage in the moment, they do not always help you to clearly signal what you need from your person, and this is where problems can arise.

It is normal to have a range of attachment strategies, some that might be considered "secure" and some that might be termed "insecure." Different relationships can call for different attachment strategies. It is important to remember that the attachment strategies you use do not define you. They are simply your range of coping strategies that help you to navigate your emotions in your most important

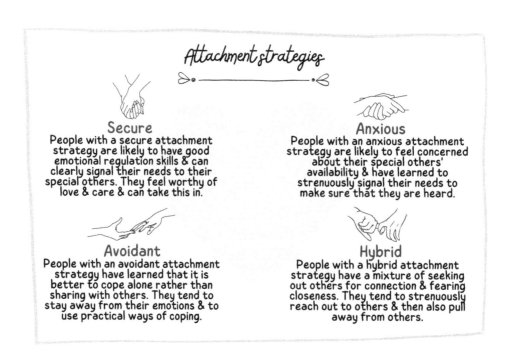

Figure 4.7 Attachment strategies.

relationships. Some will be more helpful to you than others. You will most probably find that the attachment strategies you use do not fall neatly into a specific category of "secure" or "insecure," but that you have a unique combination of strategies that you have learned over time.

Exercise 4.3

Which attachment strategy best describes how you signal your need and manage emotion in close relationships (circle)?

〜〜〜〜	**Secure (Riding the waves)** I am comfortable with closeness with others and I know that I can turn to my special others when I need them.
〜〜〜	**Anxious (Big waves)** I am uncertain that my special others will be there for me when I need them so I have to work hard to reach them.
―――― 〜〜〜	**Avoidant (Distant waves)** I prefer to keep my emotions to myself and to not reach out to my special others.
〜〜 〜〜	**Hybrid (Both distant and big waves)** I long to be able to trust and lean on my special others, and I am afraid of being hurt if I open my heart to them.

Connecting your emotional processing "wave style" to your attachment strategy

Notice how your most commonly used attachment strategy mirrors your "wave style" from session one?

There is an order to our experience. **The way we learned to navigate our attachment relationships early in life teaches us important lessons about how to manage our inner-worlds.** For instance, if you tend to withdraw from emotional connection with others and to cope alone, you might find that you are also a little more distant from your own emotional world (distant waves). If you learned to amplify your emotional signals to get an inconsistent caregiver to pay attention, you might notice that you have big waves of emotion in your inner world (big waves). If you learned in your closest relationships that turning to others was frightening or resulted in your being hurt, you might find that you can sometimes feel overwhelmed by the big waves of your emotions and at other times, feel protectively distant from them (hybrid waves).

Exercise 4.4

Learning about your attachment strategy/wave style gives you great clarity into how you have coped in some of your toughest moments. Remembering that our attachment strategies are coping strategies, it is important to name what triggers our coping strategies into action. Triggers are the people, places, and things that bring our coping strategies alive! Triggers are a sign that we feel overwhelmed and under-resourced. When overwhelmed, we all do things to ensure our survival (in the moment) but that probably do not serve us and our goals well in the long-term. Some common coping behaviors are yelling, going silent, being critical of others, avoiding sensitive topics with others, not being honest with others about how I feel or what I need, finding fault, and in general, reacting or over-reacting as a way of coping with a trigger. When you think of some recent times when you found yourself in your coping strategy, what behaviors were you doing? If you were a fly on the wall when you were triggered, what behaviors would you see yourself doing?

_____

_____

_____

_____

_____

_____

_____

_____

And, now, name your triggers! What is happening in your environment that feels overwhelming? Something happens that triggers your nervous system into overwhelm. For instance, "I feel overwhelmed and under-resourced when someone criticizes me." "I get reactive when someone accuses me of something." "I get overwhelmed when I don't feel heard, respected or valued." "I see my own defensiveness come alive when a loved one is defensive with me." Think back to the last few times you saw and heard yourself get reactive. What was triggering for you? Name your triggers here:

_____

_____

_____

_____

_____

_____

_____

_____

Our bodies give us initial signals when we are triggered, reactive, or overwhelmed. Our throats tighten, our chests clench, our stomachs churn. Feeling overwhelmed, even in quick moments, is hard on our nervous systems and bodies. Feeling overwhelmed in a long-term relationship is very taxing and our coping strategies may even become habitual. As you think about this process and answer the questions about the behaviors you see and hear yourself do based upon the triggers you experienced, tune into your body.

When I pay attention to my behaviors as I name my triggers, my body's initial signal to me is:

_____

_____

_____

_____

_____

_____

_____

_____

Knowing your *behaviors, triggers,* and *initial signals from your body* are the three elements to pay attention to in order to catch your coping strategy as it is happening. Catching your process as it is happening is key to learning how to interrupt it. Learning how to catch and interrupt your habitual ways of coping is an amazing accomplishment and such a sign of growth. It takes a lot of courage to focus inwardly especially when thinking back over some of our worst moments. All of us need to learn to interrupt our reactivity and our unproductive but habitual ways of coping. In the next three sessions, you will learn about the underlying emotions your body initially registered when you felt triggered. Our bodies register emotions and give us signals to orientate us towards our safety. Interestingly, when we are triggered, our habitual ways of coping with the triggers take over and we often are not aware of our body's initial signals. We would like you to take time in the next few sessions to reorient yourself to your signals of fear, anger, and other primary emotions which underlie your reactions when you are triggered. Getting to know and then befriending your deeper emotions is the key step to interrupting your reactive coping strategy over the long-term!

Figure 4.8 Catching your coping strategy.

Notes

1   Bowlby, J. (1969/1982). *Attachment and Loss: Volume 1 Attachment*. New York: Basic Books.
2   Bowlby, J. (1979). *The Making and Breaking of Affectional Bonds*. London: Tavistock.
3   Bowlby, J. (1988). *A Secure Base*. New York: Basic Books.
4   Shaver, P. R. & Hazan, C. (1988). A Biased Overview of the Study of Love. *Journal of Social and Personal Relationships*, 5(4), 473–501.
5   Johnson, S. M. (2008) *Hold Me Tight: Seven Conversations for a Lifetime of Love*. New York: Little, Brown and Company.
6   Shaver P. R. & Mikulincer, M. (2016). *Attachment in Adulthood: Structure, Dynamics and Change*, 2nd ed. New York: The Guilford Press.
7   Ainsworth, M. D. S., Blehar, M. C, Waters, E. & Wall, S. (1978). *Patterns of Attachment: Assessed in the Strange Situation and at Home*. Hillsdale, NJ: Erlbaum.
8   Bartholomew, K. & Horowitz, L. M. (1991). Attachment Styles among Young Adults: A Test of a Four-category Model. *Journal of Personality and Social Psychology*, 61, 226–244.

Part II

Going Deeper

Facing fear

As you start Part Two of this workbook, let us take a minute to pause and reflect on some of your key learnings that you are bringing with you from Part One. Session One was all about getting to know your general emotional processing style and what activities bring you comfort. As you continue on this journey, it remains important to care for yourself with compassion and grace. In the second session, you bravely reflected on your most recent relationship loss while you started naming your feelings from this loss. As you now know, naming your feelings is the first step toward knowing and shrinking them. The focus of Session Three was your most recent relationship's cycle of distress. In the third session, you named how you were likely to turn up the emotional heat or turn it down in heated moments with this partner. And Session Four was focused on helping you name your attachment strategy. Attachment strategies, for each of us, are based on your best coping strategy when you did not get the responsiveness from your loved one in your moments of need. It is important to remember that we each have an attachment strategy that serves two important functions: to manage our emotions in the moment and to protect us from further hurt. Each of these functions is regularly needed to ensure our well-being and sometimes needed to ensure our survival. Key elements of our coping strategies are the triggers we experience, the way our bodies respond to these triggers, and then behaviors we see ourselves doing in these difficult moments to cope with the triggers.

Central to these coping strategy moments is our fear. Most of us do not know that our fear plays such a pivotal role in our day-to-day lives and especially in our moments of stress, distress, and need. In this session, we want to orientate you to the essential role of fear, how our fear operates to insist upon our survival, and the importance of befriending our fears.

Our relationship to fear

All of us, cradle to grave, have fear. Contrary to popular belief, it is not a childhood trait to outgrow. Developing a working relationship with our fear is, ideally, a task of young adulthood. Most of us, however, never got the guidance on how to develop a working relationship with our fear as we were growing into adulthood, unfortunately. So, now, it is a task for all of us adults who realize that we do not know our own fear – especially after a major life event like losing a most important relationship. It is too bad that our schooling did not include basic courses on relationships and emotions, particularly on fear since it may be the first emotion of the emotional part of the brain (limbic brain). After all, fear originates from the startle response from the oldest part of our brains (reptilian brain)!

From an idealistic perspective, our caregivers, parents, and other adults in our young lives would have reflected our fear for us as it was happening in the moment. Naming our fears is the start of taming our fears[1]. When a caring, safe other reflects our experiences or part of our experience, it is soothing to our brains. Their reflections name our experiences for us (often when we are too young to know how to name our experience for ourselves) which breaks our isolation and starts to help us create a working relationship with our emotions, particularly fear. Literally, their words provide soothing for us even if their words are not perfectly accurate, attuned, or they are not aware of the depth of our fear and suffering. Isolation is so costly to humans. Physical isolation is absolutely taxing. Being alone physically is hard on our nervous systems for sure. In fact, we are only just beginning to understand the cost of emotional isolation on the human nervous system which is 100% wired for connection with safe others. When we are isolated emotionally, the brain has to work extra hard to ensure our survival (more on this in Session Eight: Healing Scars). It is *something* to have a safe other

DOI: 10.4324/9781003360506-8

physically present, but simply being physically present is not enough to provide emotional safety and connection, qualities the human brain is constantly needing and seeking.

When the brain has emotional connection with a safe other, it operates most efficiently. Inherent in all emotion is a metabolic load which is the load or weight of a particular emotion on our nervous systems. When the brain feels, perceives, or judges that it is alone, the weight of the emotional load increases and becomes more of a burden on the rest of the nervous system. These extra burdens (holding emotion by myself) slow the processing of emotion and inhibits the brain's processing efficiency.

When an emotion is shared with a safe other, the metabolic load of the emotion decreases. Most of us think that if we share our emotions, we will be burdening our friends and family. In reality, when we share our emotions, the sharing shrinks the metabolic load of those emotions within our own brains and does not shift the metabolic burden over to our loved ones. Because the skull limits the space for the brain (our actual gray matter), the systems within the brain have to work very efficiently. As a result, the brain has to triage available resources between parts of the brain depending on where in the brain resources are needed. The more alone we feel, the harder the brain has to work to manage the resources and send our limited resources to the right place at the right time. Due to the limitations of the skull, the brain has to pick and choose which part of the brain needs the resources the most (to ensure our survival). When we have a safe other we can share with, this sharing shrinks the load of our emotions which decreases the brain's need for triaging. As a result of sharing with a safe other, our brains work most efficiently and effectively.[2]

None of us like to face our fear. It is daunting, uncomfortable, and inconvenient. Most of us can easily say that there just is not enough time in the day to spend time facing our fears. Our nervous systems, though, never get a break from fear since fear is our human threat signaling system. Our nervous systems are constantly evaluating our environments to ensure our safety and our survival. This is our survival imperative and it happens *below* and *behind* our awareness[3]. We each have a built-in threat-scanning system that will scan for threats to ensure our survival. This will kick in whether we think we need to be worried or afraid or not. We all want to be more emotionally intelligent. Finding our fear, knowing our fear, allows us to access the *intelligence* embedded in our fear specifically and in all of our emotions. Finding our fear and befriending it is the most efficient way to trust it, contain it and, ultimately, shrink it.

Exercise 5.1

Thinking back over your life, who did you share your fears with?

_____

_____

_____

_____

Who has shared their fears with you?

_____

_____

_____

_____

As adults, life requires us to get to know ourselves emotionally, especially get to know our fear since it has an outsized role in ensuring our survival. Not only do our emotions orientate us to our safety from a survival perspective, emotions shared are the glue that keeps loved ones feeling connected to each other. The absence of emotional sharing is the death knell to love relationships.

Facing fear and shame: The why and the how

When you think back to your most recent relationship, you may wonder why we have a session focused on helping you find and befriend your fear. Is it not the point, after all, to live a life without fear or to spend your life avoiding fear? Many of our world leaders, teachers, coaches, and parents have taught us that we should not be afraid. Of course, nobody likes to be afraid – we feel small, helpless, and vulnerable when we are scared. And, if you happen to be scared, we've all been told not to admit to being afraid. Admitting fear is childish and makes us look weak, or so we have been told.

The hard part about trying to ignore or avoid our fear is how important our fear is to our humanness. Since fear lives deep in our nervous systems, humans need fear to prompt protective action. For humans – all mammals, in fact – our fear is orientating. Our fear organizes us to ensure our safety. Safety is the preeminent concern of all humans[4]. In order to help ourselves create safety, we need a relationship to our fear, which may sound paradoxical. Knowing our fears is how we orientate ourselves and our loved ones to safety.

Exercise 5.2

Getting to know your fear

When you read the words above – getting to know your fear – pay attention to your body for a moment. What is the feeling tone your body has when you think of getting to know your fear? Some people describe it as dread. Others find and feel relief. What is the tone inside you when you think about getting to know your fear?

_____

_____

_____

_____

General Fears

Close your eyes and let yourself think about your fear. General fears like "I am afraid of heights or snakes or drowning." Write your general fears:

_____

_____

_____

_____

_____

As you write and read your general fears, what emotions do you feel? What starts to stir on the inside of you?

_____

_____

_____

_____

_____

Relationship Fears

Closing your eyes again, think about the fears you have about important relationships in your life. Take some deep breaths and let yourself name your relationship fears such as "I'll always be a disappointment," "I am afraid she/he/they will leave me," or "I am afraid I am not worthy of love." As you think about your relationship fears, write them here:

_____

_____

_____

_____

_____

As you write and read your relationship fears, what do you feel? What emotions start to come alive on the inside of you?

_____

_____

_____

_____

_____

Most recent relationship fears

And, lastly, your fears related to this most recent relationship…what fears do you have about this most recent relationship? Fears about mistakes made in that relationship, fears about not knowing what went wrong in this relationship or fears about being unsure of how to heal and grow from this important relationship are all possible. Take a moment to think about this most recent relationship and its ending. What fears do you have?

_____

_____

_____

_____

And, as you write these fears, you feel what is stirring on the inside? What emotion is coming alive for you?

_____

_____

_____

_____

Thinking back to the "waves styles" from Session One, what are some signs to look out for that you are getting overwhelmed by big waves of your fear and might need to take a break from them?

_____

_____

_____

_____

_____

_____

What are some signs to look out for that you might be avoiding touching your fears and might need to lean in a little closer to them?

_____

_____

_____

_____

_____

_____

Exercise 5.3

What do you do with your fear?

For decades, the science has been clear that the behaviors people do when feeling fear (action tendencies) are to fight or take flight. When a human (or mammal, for that matter) feels fear, the body moves in predictable ways to gain safety and protection. Science reveals that we would fight or take flight as a way of coping with fear and ensuring survival. Blood rushes to our limbs to ready us for either action. Some examples of fighting as a way to cope with fear are to make yourself bigger physically, to impose yourself and go closer to the threat, or to get louder. Some examples of taking flight are avoiding the threat by backing up and going in another direction, making yourself small, or going quiet. When you feel fear, what does your body do? What behaviors do you see yourself do when you are afraid?

_____

_____

_____

Some of these behaviors may look defensive or be protective, understandably. Defenses play important roles in our moments of fear and pain. All humans use defenses as a way of protecting ourselves and our vulnerabilities. Defenses are protection of our vulnerabilities. An unfortunate aspect of defensiveness, though, is that being defensive pushes our loved ones away. While defenses serve to protect us, at times, these same defenses keep us isolated, disconnected, and alone just when we need connection and reassurance the most.

What defenses do you use when you are vulnerable? Do you go on the attack (fight) with your words, tone or loudness? Do you try to hide and deny your role (take flight)? Write your typical defenses here:

_____

_____

_____

_____

_____

_____

Exercise 5.4

First fear, then need

Underneath our fear and defensiveness is our need. So few of our caregivers asked us what we needed when we were afraid. Most just told us not to be afraid or to stop being so silly, irritational, or weak when we shared our fear. Many told us that there was nothing to be afraid of despite our own bodies feeling afraid. How is this for the start of not trusting our own feelings and bodily sensations when they alert us to something important happening in our environments?

Now that you are developing a working relationship with your fear and you are starting to be able to name the behaviors you use to cope with your fear (including defenses), we invite you to think about what might be your underlying need when you are afraid? Many of us need to hear that our fear makes sense, that all of us have fear even when we are high-functioning, successful adults, and that it is okay – even important – to pay attention to our fears. Sometimes our needs are behavioral; sometimes they are emotional. Sometimes they are both behavioral and emotional: do not leave me alone when I am scared, for instance.

If you take a look at Figure 5.1, Iceberg of experience, you can see that what we show above the surface is often not the whole story. Beneath our reactive, defensive behaviors and emotions, there is typically a wealth of experience that includes our softer feelings and our needs. For instance, when

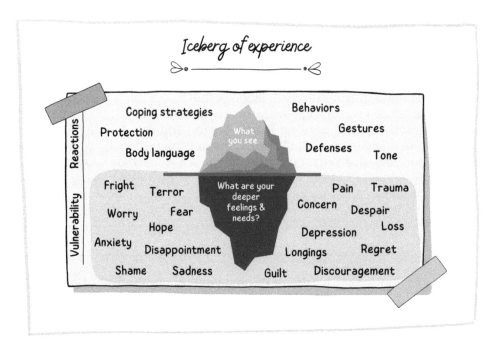

Figure 5.1 Iceberg of experience.

someone displays defensive protective behaviors on the surface, they might be actually feeling sad or hurt or scared underneath. They might really be needing reassurance or comfort, but this is usually not clear in their actions.

When you were afraid in your last relationship, what were you needing underneath?

_____

_____

_____

_____

_____

_____

When you feel afraid now, what are you needing most?

_____

_____

_____

_____

_____

_____

What reassuring words do you need to hear from the special people in your life? What do you need from your loved ones when you are afraid?

_____

_____

_____

_____

_____

_____

Exercise 5.5

Fight, flight and now freeze

In more recent years, when fighting and taking flight do not offer or provide us with enough protection or get us to safety, the latest science has revealed another action tendency for fear: to freeze/go immobile[5]. When we see something scary or feel afraid and we cannot cope by fighting or taking flight, we can freeze. Our breath gets shallow, our bodies stop moving and our limbs go numb. In the moment of fear or fright, this freezing allows us to survive. Think of a mouse "playing dead" in a cat's mouth. The cat thinks it has caught its next meal until the cat drops the mouse and the mouse runs away! Humans sometimes need to cope in this way too. We submit or appease – go immobile – to deal with danger. It is our survival instinct/imperative telling us how to cope to increase our chances for survival in our worst moments. Sometimes, we notice that we can freeze temporarily when faced with a surprise or a scary situation. Think of a young child running, tripping, and falling. Most of us would freeze temporarily before jumping into action to soothe the child.

Have you noticed that you freeze when surprised or that you have ever gone immobile as a way to cope with fear? If so, write what you remember from this moment:

_____

_____

_____

_____

As you have started to befriend your fear, let us focus for a few minutes on where your fear lives in your body. For all of us, our emotions form the bedrock of our sensations[6] and so our emotions literally "move" us physiologically. Lots of people tell us how their fear grips their chest or their shoulders or churns their stomachs. What is the sensation of your fear and where does it come alive in your body?

_____

_____

_____

_____

In Figure 5.2, you can see a typical process of moving from more superficial (but not trivial) emotions to the deeper ones. All of us need to regularly find our deeper emotions in order to really get to know ourselves and especially our fears. If we do not know ourselves at a deeper emotional level, we will be missing all the intelligence that lives in these deeper layers!

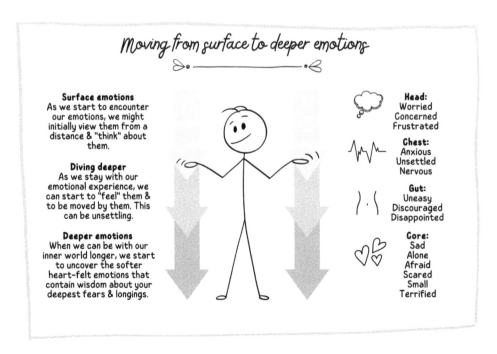

Figure 5.2 Moving from surface to deeper emotions.

Exercise 5.6

As you continue getting to know your fear, let us talk about healthy ways humans process their fear. The first part of processing fear, as you know, is to name it. Naming is the first action we can take which starts to distill our fear. We continue to distill our fear by tracking how it comes alive (what is the trigger?), where it comes alive in our bodies (chest, shoulders/neck, stomach/gut, in our throats, etc.), what the voice of our fear says to us about us and about others (you are not getting it right, do not make another mistake, be leery, do not trust, others are out to get you, etc.).

Some healthy ways of processing your fear: there is sharing with a loved one who can empathize and reassure you, there is walking in nature where sometimes we talk to ourselves to process the fear, there is crying to release the emotional pressure embedded in the fear, there are healthy distractions like listening to soothing music, exercising, watching your favorite show, writing to yourself in your journal, and having fun with a good friend or a loved one.

Remembering your wave style here can really help you to know how to best meet your fear and to process it.

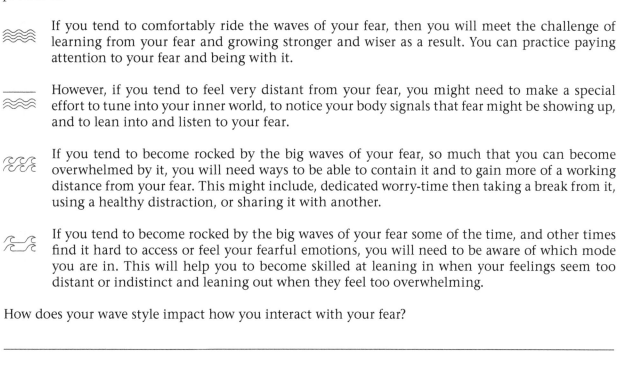

If you tend to comfortably ride the waves of your fear, then you will meet the challenge of learning from your fear and growing stronger and wiser as a result. You can practice paying attention to your fear and being with it.

However, if you tend to feel very distant from your fear, you might need to make a special effort to tune into your inner world, to notice your body signals that fear might be showing up, and to lean into and listen to your fear.

If you tend to become rocked by the big waves of your fear, so much that you can become overwhelmed by it, you will need ways to be able to contain it and to gain more of a working distance from your fear. This might include, dedicated worry-time then taking a break from it, using a healthy distraction, or sharing it with another.

If you tend to become rocked by the big waves of your fear some of the time, and other times find it hard to access or feel your fearful emotions, you will need to be aware of which mode you are in. This will help you to become skilled at leaning in when your feelings seem too distant or indistinct and leaning out when they feel too overwhelming.

How does your wave style impact how you interact with your fear?

_____

_____

_____

_____

_____

What are some healthy ways of processing your fear:

_____

_____

_____

_____

_____

_____

Figure 5.3 Notes on fear.

As necessary for all of our emotions, in order to get the intelligence from our fear, we must befriend it. Most of us make meaning about our fear and other emotions too quickly. Actually, we try to make meaning before the emotion has had a chance to move us to safety - the literal role of emotion. Our hunch is that good people try to make meaning quickly thinking that it will make their fear go away or make their pain hurt less. In fact, the opposite is true! As you have learned in this session, naming, going closer to your fear and then sharing it with a safe other are the fastest ways to contain, shrink, and dissipate the fear!

About panic attacks

Many of us have panic attacks which are overwhelming, scary, and very unsettling. Panic attacks feel like intense waves of big emotion, a tsunami of emotions, or an unwelcome, uncontrollable vibration throughout our bodies. Panic attacks can also make us "go blank," feel numb, or disassociate from our bodily sensations. During panic attacks, people often report feeling outside themselves and their bodies, floating above their bodies, or zoned out and not aware of their bodies. The essence of panic attacks are signals and sensations of overwhelming emotion that can no longer stay bottled, suppressed, or pushed away. As a phenomenon, emotion is too potent and too necessary for survival to suppress or keep at a distance. Panic attacks occur when there is a back-log of unprocessed emotion that comes over us, overwhelms us or surprises us.

The best way to manage panic attacks is to stay up-to-date with your emotional experiences! Easy to say and hard to do especially when faced with the overwhelming pain of a lost love relationship. Having a regular practice of finding and befriending your feelings is the best way to prevent panic attacks from forming or happening. Panic attacks are also more likely to happen when we feel at our worst or are under-resourced. Maybe we struggle with depression or anxiety which fuels the fire of panic attacks. Perhaps we are exhausted and sleep deprived which can make panic attacks more likely.

If you suffer from panic attacks, what are the typical triggers for you?

_____

_____

_____

_____

_____

_____

_____

Describe what you are aware of when a panic attack is happening for you:

_____

_____

_____

_____

_____

_____

_____

During and/or immediately after a panic attack, what would be soothing for you?

_____

_____

_____

_____

_____

_____

_____

_____

A note about shame

When we start to befriend our fears and uncover our needs, many of us will also feel shame since life and adulthood has conditioned us to feel ashamed about our fears, needs and responses to them. Shame is an often misunderstood soup of emotions that usually serves a defensive function. None of us got enough assistance from our loved ones to help us understand and work with our own shame. We would like to help you get to know your shame too in this session!

The neurological underpinnings of shame

A hit of shame acts as impulse control just like hitting the brakes on your car to slow it[7]. We use shame to slow ourselves in order to prevent further exposure (relationship exposure) when additional exposure could lead to more rejection or hurt. In order to avoid additional rejection from our loved ones, we will use shame to inhibit ourselves. We stop ourselves (often with blame and negative self-talk) as a way to limit our exposure to more pain and rejection. One of the key ways that shame is adaptive is when shame inhibits us from seeking reassurance or acceptance from important others when it is likely that they will not support or reassure us. When this happens, we blame ourselves with negative self-talk as a way to bring about our shame which keeps us safe. When we blame ourselves, at least the locus of control resides within us, which is better than feeling the helplessness of having no control at all. Shame and blame go hand-in-hand. By blaming ourselves, we have control over ourselves which is mobilizing and provides pseudo-empowerment as compared to not having control over our parents, caregivers, teachers, and other important adults in our lives which leaves us feeling so helpless. And, as we grow and more clearly see the limitations of our loved ones, it is not unusual to hear yourself blame them as well for their lacks and limitations. The voice of shame has a circularity. We send negative messages to ourselves about ourselves which we internalize, use to be hard on ourselves, and to keep ourselves small. At times, we turn this blame toward others as a way to not feel like we are the only faulty one. Their reactions to us and our blame often confirms those negative messages, unfortunately. The circularity of shame and blame not only plays out inside of us but also plays a role in perpetuating these negative messages between us and our loved ones.

The costly part about shame, though, is that we start believing that the voice of shame is true and that the shame and its voice are us rather than a voice of our pain from enduring. Most of us think the shame (or the voice of shame) is us. Most of us believe the voice of shame: we are bad, defective, not worthy, we do not have what it takes, we constantly make mistakes, we are unlovable. After coping this way for years, we have lost track of the original purpose of evoking shame: *to protect us from further rejection*. We do not know or realize that the feeling of shame was initially there to serve a protective function. Once we start believing that the voice of our shame is us and we do not have a loved one offering perspective and antidote messages, our voice of shame begins to feel like a prison. The protection of a hit of shame was intended to prevent further relationship rejection but now the voice of "protection" sounds like/feels like the voice of imprisonment.

Exercise 5.7

Like with fear, shame too has a common predictable response and that is to hide. Humans respond in predictable ways to the basic emotions that all people have and the action tendency response for shame is to hide: hide from others, hide parts of myself from myself, hide from life.

What does the voice of your shame say? What messages does your shame give you?

_____

_____

_____

_____

What beliefs about yourself are fueled by your shame?

_____

_____

_____

_____

How does your shame want/compel you to behave?

_____

_____

_____

_____

In working with your shame, we want to help you unpack the emotions embedded in your shame. If your shame is a soup of emotions, what are the emotional ingredients such as sadness, fear, anger?

Exercise 5.8

These exercises on naming the voices of your shame and writing the words that your shame says are the start of wedging[8] yourself between you and your shame. This is a start to realizing that you are not your shame. The voices of shame are not you! It is really important to continue to externalize the voices of your shame.

Just like wearing a pair of glasses, shame can alter how we view the world, ourselves and others. To gain a working distance from this part of your left-over, residual pain, we would like to invite you to separate your view of yourself from the negative, shaming messages you might have received about yourself throughout your life. In stepping back a little from these shaming messages, and seeing that they are not reflections of reality, but a lens through which we see things, this can help you to separate yourself a little.

Take a look at Figure 5.4 and see if you can step back from the shaming messages you have learned about yourself and your worth throughout your life.

What could you remind yourself of to create separation between the lens and you? For most of us, we need to imagine what a benevolent caregiver would have said to us. We need to picture in our mind a loving, gentle and wise caregiver soothing us with their words of wisdom. E.g. "It was not my fault that my caregivers were not available for me;" "I did nothing to deserve that;" "I am worthy of love and care without having to earn it;" "others in my life have responded warmly to me;" "I deserve to be loved." Take a deep breath in and listen to your heart. What words does your heart long to hear in order to antidote the voices of shame that have inhibited you?

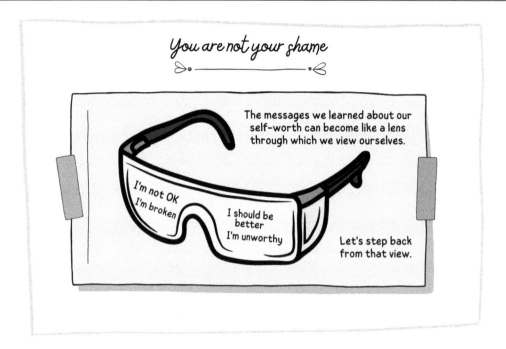

Figure 5.4 You are not your shame.

As we wrap up this session, we encourage you to take some time to care for yourself. This was an intense session. There is a lot to process in order to make space for and go closer to our fears. It is intense to go closer to our fears especially since most of us are taught or told to get away from our fears and avoid them at all cost! Now, take some deep breaths, tell yourself how proud you are of yourself, and thank yourself for your courage. You have continued to do really important work in growing from your fear, pain, and loss. We are so proud of you!

Notes

1 Siegel, D. J. and Payne Bryson, T. (2011). *The Whole-Brain Child: 12 Revolutionary Strategies to Nurture Your Child's Developing Mind*. New York: Random House.
2 Coan, J. A. (2008). Toward a neuroscience of attachment. In J. Cassidy & P. R. Shaver (Eds.), *Handbook of Attachment: Theory, Research, and Clinical Applications* (pp. 241–265). The Guilford Press.
3 Porges, S. (2016). *Presentation at Psychotherapy Networker Symposium*, Washington, D.C.
4 de Becker, G. (1997). *The Gift of Fear: Survival Signals that Protect Us from Violence*. New York: Little, Brown and Company.
5 Porges, S. (2016). Presentation at *Psychotherapy Networker Symposium*, Washington, D.C.
6 Levine, P. (2010). *In an Unspoken Voice: How the Body Releases Trauma and Restores Goodness*. Berkeley, CA: North Atlantic Books.
7 Schore, A. (2015). *Affect Regulation and the Origin of the Self*. New York: Routledge.
8 Fisher, J. (2018). *Presentation at the Psychotherapy Networker Symposium*, Washington, D.C.

Riding the waves of anger

Last session was focused on getting to know your fear since fear constantly orientates us to our survival. In this session, Session Six, we will be focusing on helping you to get to know your anger, especially since most of us do not have a relationship with our own anger and might not want one. Yet, anger too has intelligence we need! We want to help you learn to ride the waves of your anger because that is what it takes to glean intelligence from and to transform anger.

Anger is arguably the biggest emotion that humans experience although most of us do not understand the phenomenon of anger. Many of us try to transform our anger by denying it or by thinking "rationally" about it. If only those strategies worked! We know how uncomfortable unprocessed anger is. It is such a big emotion that the body has a hard time holding it in. In fact, unprocessed anger is very hard to contain and, as a result, often comes out in ways that are painful, destructive, and scary for others. These are some of the reasons why anger has such a bad rap. Its negative reputation comes from the scary behaviors, including aggression, that many see and associate with anger.

Anger, at its essence, is a beacon for change. Once we know this, we can find the protest in our anger. Since humans do not get angry for no reason (the brain is too risk-averse to get angry for no reason, but more on this later), there's always a protest that needs to be spoken, validated, and respected in order for the strength of the anger to start diminishing. Anger gets repetitive and hard to hold when it has not been heard and validated. In this session, we will help you find and name the protest in your anger and learn how to express your anger in safe and productive ways. There is a purity and an energy within our anger that is the beacon for change!

Anger is one of the hardest emotions to process and to make sense of. It is big and strong and regularly misunderstood. Anger gets its bad reputation from people who have been understandably angry but behaved badly and, at times, aggressively, as a result. Read your local headlines and unfortunately you will read about humans being destructive as a result of being angry. Most of us associate anger with reactivity, aggression, and even revenge. But, at its essence, anger is just another regular, understandable human experience. All humans experience anger although nobody has helped us learn much about it or what to do with it. Typically, as we are growing up, nobody helped us work with our anger in ways that teach us about it. This is an important piece of humanity and "emotions 101" that has not been taught. Believe it or not, anger has a bunch of intelligence embedded in it for us – just like every other emotion.

Exercise 6.1

Growing up, what messages did you receive about anger in general? How was it expressed (or not)?

_____

_____

_____

_____

_____

DOI: 10.4324/9781003360506-9

Figure 6.1 Notes on anger.

What messages did you get from your family about your anger?

_____

_____

_____

_____

_____

_____

As you are no doubt noticing, we learn powerful lessons about emotions, particularly anger, from our families. These experiences shape how we experience our emotions and how we express them to others. In this session, we are providing an overview of the important role of anger, we will break down the elements of anger, and then we will help you get to know your anger so that you can benefit from the wisdom embedded in it.

The function of anger

As you know, anger is a complex and often misunderstood emotion. Anger is a complicated emotional phenomenon which makes it hard to contain and hard to work with. For all of us, it is hard to hold anger. As a result of the unwieldiness of anger, the associated action tendencies (behaviors) humans employ to cope with and manage anger are required to be big. The actions of anger are to assert or defend. *Assert or defend*: big movements from our bodies to protect us and to ensure our survival. Humans have needed to assert or defend themselves to ensure their survival time and time again. When our personal space has been intruded upon, we assert ourselves. When our boundaries have been violated, we defend ourselves and re-establish those boundaries. When we feel exploited, we defend. Anger is a mobilizing emotion. Like pain, anger demands to be felt. Our anger becomes demanding, especially the more it is denied or repressed. Anger has mobilized humans to take action across our lifespans and for centuries.

Our anger is literally meant to move us by asserting or defending in order to ensure our survival. Anger protects and moves us away from danger. Anger moves us to take action toward our safety. Anger insists upon action and is seldom ignored. Because of the inherent movement of anger as a phenomenon, it is extremely hard to contain. Most of us think that if we suppress our anger, it will go away. If we bottle it up or sweep it under the rug, it will dissipate. The reality is that anger, like all other strong emotions, is very hard to suppress. Suppression is meant to be employed as a short-term strategy to cope with an emergency. Suppression can work in isolated, short-term crises only. Since suppression works in some contexts, many of us try to apply it across other, broader contexts. Using suppression as a regular coping strategy is difficult and comes at a cost to us. Essentially, humans are not wired to suppress emotion. It is costly to the human nervous system to use suppression strategies regularly. Shutting down emotionally does not calm us down, unfortunately[1].

Humans express emotions regularly whether we want to or not. Our bodies insist on this strategy since our survival depended on a caregiver caring for us when we were young, small, and dependent. Our faces contract in characteristic ways depending on our emotional states. Our voice tone shifts along with our emotions. Our body movements and gestures change too as a result of our emotions. So, whether or not we are aware of our emotions, or want them or not, our physiology is already wired for us to feel and share our emotions. Emotions are built-in signaling system! Since emotions do not stay in our skin and, in fact, they seep out of every pore, the vastness of anger especially is really hard to keep inside.

Exercise 6.2

What behaviors have you seen others use to cope when they are angry?

_____

_____

_____

_____

_____

What behaviors have you used to cope when you are angry?

_____

_____

_____

_____

_____

How did it feel to see others' behaviors when they were angry?

_____

_____

_____

_____

_____

How does it feel to name your behaviors when you have been angry?

_____

_____

_____

_____

_____

Thinking back to the "waves styles" from earlier sessions, what memories do you have of getting overwhelmed by big waves of your anger or other people's anger?

_____

_____

_____

_____

_____

What are some signs to look out for that you might be avoiding touching your angry feelings and might need to lean in a little closer to hear the message in them?

_____

_____

_____

_____

_____

If you notice that you can sometimes feel engulfed by your angry feelings and then at other times feel really numbed to them, what do you tend to do in each mode?

_____

_____

_____

_____

_____

Are there ever times when you can ride the waves of your anger in a way that allows you to listen to the message in them without being engulfed by them? If so, what is this like for you? What stands out for you about these times?

_____

_____

_____

As we have said before, people do not get angry for no reason! So let us slow down and look at one of the most recent times you felt angry. Maybe think about one of the scenarios or memories you wrote about in the preceding exercise. Pay attention to what it was that triggered your anger. Triggers are changes in our environment. Triggers orientate us to something new, different, uncomfortable, or unsafe.

Exercise 6.3

When you think back to a recent time when you were angry, what was the trigger?

_____

_____

_____

_____

_____

_____

As you track back to when this trigger occurred, what did you say to yourself? What do you remember thinking about this new situation?

_____

_____

_____

_____

_____

_____

Triggers force us to appraise our situation. We assess the situation from a perspective of, "Am I safe?" When you think back to this trigger, what was your initial appraisal of the situation? To help with this question, it might help to know that this moment is all about survival; initial appraisals are general thoughts such as "Oh no, this situation is bad, wrong, or unsafe." What did you say to yourself? If you do not remember thinking anything to yourself when this event occurred, what would you say to yourself now if this event just happened a minute ago?

_____

_____

_____

_____

_____

_____

When your anger was triggered and you noticed the thoughts you had, how did your body respond? People talk about feeling their anger come alive, get big/expand/amplify, fill their chests, grow like a tsunami, come in waves, as examples. What sensations did your body have? How did your body respond?

_____

_____

_____

_____

_____

And, what is an image that is a good representation of your anger?

_____

_____

_____

_____

_____

Then, as you stay with this memory of a recent time when you felt angry, what meaning did you make about yourself or others? People say things like "I knew I shouldn't have trusted;" "I knew it was too good to be true;" "I should have trusted myself;" "I should have listened to my gut/doubt;" "they had no right;" "they were wrong," as examples. Write the meaning you made about yourself and others who were involved:

_____

_____

_____

_____

_____

Finally, what action did you take in this situation? You might have stayed silent or walked away or you might have spoken up and let your protest be heard. What do you remember doing behaviorally as a way to cope with this situation?

_____

_____

_____

As you complete this exercise, notice now how you are feeling. What sensations have come alive in your body? What is tight; what is relieved? Breathe into the feeling of tightness, relief, or what word best fits your experience. In order to experience our emotions, we have to slow down to make contact with them. As you slow down now by breathing into your body's sensations, what feelings come alive for you?

_____

_____

_____

_____

_____

_____

Anger is a beacon for change

At its essence, our anger is a beacon for change. Anger comes alive regularly because we are human and aspects of life do not feel good to us. When something does not feel good, it impacts us emotionally. When something does not feel good perpetually, it understandably makes us angry. Anger is repetitive when it is denied, dismissed or trivialized. When we notice the repetition in our anger or even being angry about a situation for the first time, it is up to each of us to wonder about and start to name the change that our anger is fueling/urging/compelling in us. Embedded in all of our anger is a protest. Anger calls for us to pay attention. It implores us to ask: what is the need embedded in our anger?

Exercise 6.4

Most of us do not live with enough relational support to slow our anger, find the protest within it, and share it in a vulnerable way. It takes time and effort, but it is worth it to name and voice the protest embedded in your anger _for_ yourself _with_ yourself initially.

Some examples of things that our anger can be pointing out for us are (tick the ones that apply to you):

- That our rights or boundaries are being violated
- That there is an injustice
- That we are unheard
- That our emotions or needs are invalidated/ignored/dismissed
- That we are in pain
- That we are scared
- That we feel not good enough
- That we feel invisible
- That we feel helpless and powerless
- That we are disappointed or let down
- That the world is unpredictable and frightening
- That we are being treated unfairly
- That we are being threatened or hurt
- That we are being held-back, restricted or controlled

More: _____

_____

_____

_____

_____

What is your anger protesting? What does the voice of your protest need to say?

_____

_____

_____

_____

_____

_____

_____

Since anger is truly a beacon for change, what is the change your anger is compelling you to do, to change, to fight for? What does your anger need?

_____

_____

_____

_____

_____

_____

_____

_____

A note about resentment

Resentment is a soup of different emotions: anger, frustration, annoyance, irritation, hurt, and sadness, among others. When we notice our resentment, it usually indicates that there is a backlog of unprocessed and unexpressed emotion. Resentment is a common outcome of suppression and it usually starts small. With continued suppression, however, small resentments grow and grow until they overflow into an outburst of some sort. It is a pile-up of emotions that ends up weighing us down and clogging our emotional systems. When we have an over-reaction or an outburst (all humans have them!), it usually means there is some resentment related to the situation that brought about the over-reaction. When we have a short fuse with someone, it can be another sign that we have a build-up of resentment. When we have trouble feeling or being empathic or compassionate toward important others, it can be a sign that we have resentment. Resentment builds quite easily in good people. It is the simple outcome of unprocessed anger, pain and other unexpressed emotions.

Exercise 6.5

To whom or what do you have resentment toward? What situations do you resent?

_____

_____

_____

_____

_____

_____

What is a good image that reflects your resentment?

_____

_____

_____

_____

_____

_____

What are the emotions in your soup of resentment (e.g. hurt, anger, fear, sadness, disappointment, discouragement)?

_____

_____

_____

_____

_____

Can you let yourself feel some of those emotions now? If so, slow your breathing and find where these emotions live inside you. Where inside yourself does your resentment live?

_____

_____

_____

_____

_____

What is it like to feel some of these emotions now?

_____

_____

_____

_____

_____

What has prevented you from processing your emotions that built up into this resentment?

_____

_____

_____

_____

_____

Two types of anger

Some emotions function to protect us in our moments of vulnerability, threat, or danger. These emotions are defensive in nature since defenses provide protection. When in need of protection, our emotions are fast-moving, reactive, and "hard" in nature. While not trivial at all, these reactive emotions are more on the surface or more superficial. They are quick to emerge and aim to keep us safe in the short-term. We call the fast-moving anger "secondary reactive anger" because it is protecting something vulnerable or defending against something that does not feel good. Anger is a common reactive emotion for all humans. While common, secondary reactive anger is hard on relationships. When we share and receive reactive anger with our loved ones, they will usually feel blamed, criticized, or attacked. Obviously, we know that this can create damage to our closest bonds. Most of us do not know that there is a softer feeling connected to a vulnerability underneath this surface level, hard reaction.

The other type of anger is the "softer," deeper anger that is connected to our human vulnerabilities and can be shared without blame. This non-blaming anger is closest to the heart of the matter, which makes us feel vulnerable and more exposed. That is why it feels so hard to share softer anger. There is a purity and simplicity to our deeper, softer anger. When we share this softer, more distilled, non-blaming anger with a loved one, they usually lean in and want to support us. We call this "primary adaptive anger" because it comes from the heart of our most vulnerable emotions and it is adaptive when shared softly (as in, it helps us to get our needs met). This kind of anger is like a calm, firm assertion of needs and expressing it helps us to make movement in the direction of what matters most to us. Many of us have a hard time sharing soft anger because we feel so open and vulnerable doing this. It is hard to feel vulnerable when we feel angry! It is very different to let ourselves feel both angry _and_ vulnerable. I often ask myself to whisper my anger as a way to get in touch with my vulnerable anger. If you have a look at Figure 6.2, you will see the relationship of primary and secondary anger.

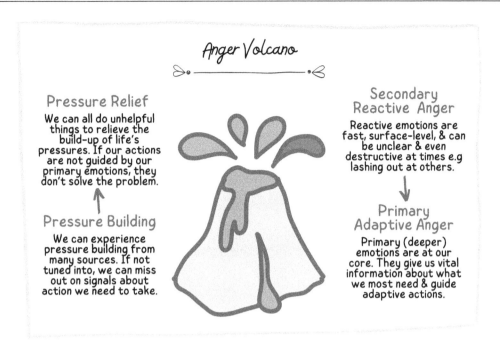

Figure 6.2 Anger volcano.

Exercise 6.6

How do you express your more surface, defensive anger?

_____

_____

_____

_____

_____

_____

What do you think might be at the core of your primary, softer anger? What could be the deeper need that is crying out to be heard?

_____

_____

_____

_____

_____

_____

_____

How do you express your deeper, softer anger?

_____

_____

_____

_____

_____

_____

What do you need to express and share more vulnerably when you are angry? How could those closest to you help you feel brave enough to share your anger vulnerably?

_____

_____

_____

_____

_____

_____

Have a look at Figure 6.3 and read through the lists of healthy and unhealthy ways that people can express their anger. This is a summary of how to grow your awareness about whether you are experiencing reactive, surface anger or softer, primary anger.

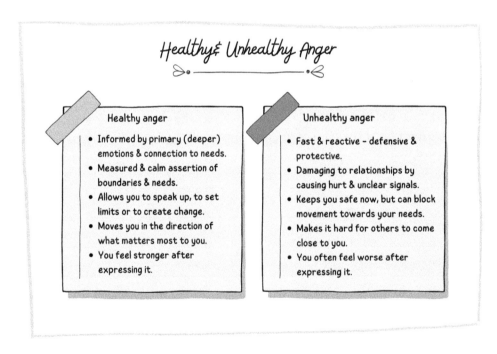

Figure 6.3 Healthy and unhealthy anger.

Tracking and slowing your anger to find the wisdom embedded in it

It is really important to remind yourself that humans do not get angry or resentful without good reasons. Even when inconvenient, unclear, or "irrational," the brain is too risk-averse to have an emotional response for no good reason. Sometimes, the hardest part is slowing down our reactions enough to find the trigger for our pain, fear and other emotions. There is always a trigger even if it is small. When we find the trigger and track our emotional process, "irrational" emotion reactions become rational, logical emotional responses. In context, our emotional responses always make sense. Initially, it can be hard to see the context but by slowing and distilling our reactivity, the context becomes clearer and ends up making sense! Since we feel with our whole bodies and our bodies are always working to ensure our survival, our emotions always make sense even if confusing initially. When our emotions do not make sense to us, it is prime time to slow them down and lean into them. Tracking your emotions, like you have done here, will bring all kinds of clarity! This is how we glean intelligence from our emotions.

Exercise 6.7

Remembering your wave style here can really help you to know how to best meet your anger and to process it. Here are some suggestions for how you can work with your anger depending on your wave style:

 If you tend to comfortably ride the waves of your anger, then you will meet the challenge of learning from your anger and growing stronger and wiser as a result. You can practice paying attention to your anger, learning from the message in it and sharing it vulnerably with safe others as needed.

 However, if you tend to feel very distant from your angry feelings, you might need to make a special effort to tune into your inner world to notice your body signals that indicate that anger might be showing up, so that you can lean into and listen to your anger in order to use it as a beacon for change.

 If you tend to become rocked by the big waves of your anger, so much that you can become overwhelmed by it, you might need to gain more of a working distance from it. This might include: catching yourself in unhelpful loops of thinking, taking a break from your emotions by using distraction, calming your physiology with calm breathing or physical exercise, or by sharing it with another.

 If you tend to become rocked by the big waves of your anger some of the time and other times find that it is far out of reach, you could benefit from paying close attention to your inner world to notice which mode you might currently be in. Then you can consciously select strategies to lean closer to your anger (such as noticing your body signals that anger might be present, making room for angry feelings and listening to the message in them) or to lean out from your anger (such as giving yourself breathing room from the intensity of your feelings by taking a break, using distraction, or calming your body).

How does your wave style impact how you interact with your anger?

_____

_____

_____

_____

_____

What would you like to do more of, or less of, in order to best tune into the message in your angry feelings and to use them in the service of your wellbeing?

_____

_____

_____

_____

_____

_____

One of the hardest things about this type of exploration is not judging yourself or anybody else. Take a moment now to reflect on the hard work you have just completed in this session. Like the previous session focused on Facing Fear, this session involving going closer to your anger is just as difficult. Maybe even more difficult, actually. How are you doing now? Take some deep breaths and acknowledge yourself, your courage, and your strength for learning how to ride the waves of your anger.

Note

1   Gross, J. (2015). *Handbook of emotional regulation* (2nd ed). New York: The Guilford Press.

Naming and healing emotional scars

Emotional scars result from emotional traumas, neglect, and ruptures. Trauma, especially when it occurs in relationships, is a crisis of connection, not an illness carried on the inside[1]. When trauma happens in a close relationship, it is not just the pain that we are left with but the shattered trust and altered expectations. Events become traumatic when we become immobilized by our fear[2] and we feel utterly alone[3]. The emotional pain of these traumatic events and violated expectations can overwhelm a person's ability to cope. This can mean that their best attempt to cope with the enormous pain means that they have to shut-off and avoid parts of their inner world – the parts that are just too dangerous to touch. As a result of trauma like this, parts of us freeze, harden, become fragmented. Echoes of trauma get stored on the inside of us and become the part of us that is always lurking in the background, on the fringes of our experience. We can desperately try to heal these parts that lurk on our own and we can often receive messages that we *should* be able to heal these parts on our own. But, despite your best efforts to heal yourself, unless your healing is done within safe and healthy relationships, you might find that you become stuck, that the pain still lurks and that it can block you from living a full and rich life. Since our self-identity forms and grows from the loving reflections we get from our most important relationships, relationships can become fertile grounds for growth and healing.[4]

A common hallmark of trauma is emotional dysregulation. Emotional dysregulation is when we feel overwhelmed or flooded and we lose our emotional balance. This happens in the moments when the painful echoes of trauma come out from the shadows and overwhelm you with their intensity. Since emotions are a constant for humans, losing our emotional balance happens for us all. However, after enduring trauma, restoring our emotional balance becomes harder and harder. Emotions naturally come alive and play out in our most important relationships. So, since emotions are always relational and trauma pushes us off-balance emotionally, our relationships can end up stressed and de-stabilized. This is never more so the case than when you have been hurt in close relationships. Why would not your fears of being hurt again come alive? As a consequence, the emotional dysregulation of trauma scrambles the emotional signals we send our loved ones, sometimes leaving our loved ones unsure of our message. We end up with one foot on the gas and another foot on the brake and that emotional push-pull is really hard on us and our relationships.

Many lyrics of country music songs, as well as messages from our earliest caregivers, have told us that time heals all wounds. If something hurts, give it time. This is certainly true to some small degree. We fall off our bicycles, time heals our wounds but only after the wound is cleaned, drained, and protected. Time does not heal wounds that are still full of debris. Wounds full of debris take a lot longer to heal. Emotional wounds have emotional debris that is just as real as gravel, rocks, and dirt. Creating the emotional environment for healing, just as we do as we clean and protect our physical injuries, allows the body to start the healing process. Actually, emotion does not care about or pay attention to time. Chronology does not influence the emotion that results from trauma. It does not care how long ago a painful or traumatic event occurred. It does not care that three or thirty years have passed. Emotions are remembered as long as they are relevant to your survival. If they are relevant, they will be remembered. So, from an emotional perspective, time does not heal emotional wounds. They can fade but not all do. Some are simply too potent and too important to our survival to fade or be forgotten.

DOI: 10.4324/9781003360506-10

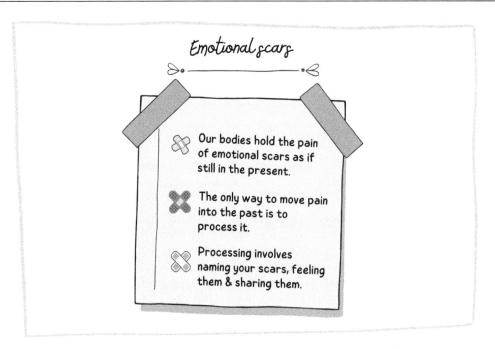

Figure 7.1 Emotional scars.

The emotional imprint of trauma

It is common knowledge that the cells of our skin and the soft tissue inside our bodies get scarred from physical injuries and traumas. Injuries to our tissues cause wounds that need time and attention to aid in the healing. Wounds often leave scars as they are healing and even long after they are healed. What is less commonly known and understood is that humans have "emotional tissue" as well. Our "emotional tissue" gets wounded as a result of injuries and traumas just like the soft tissue of our physical bodies. None of us forget what happened emotionally when we bumped a hot stove, our loved one rejected us, or an important other turned away in our big moment of need. These scars are etched into our memories and leave their own imprint just like physical scars do. Emotional imprints – a version of scars – are why emotionally-ladened memories do not fade over time like other less emotional memories.

Our brain's memory systems are designed so that typical (not emotionally overwhelming) memories fade over time because the brain needs space to store new information. Pieces of memories that are not emotionally-loaded get dropped each night as we sleep so that our brains can take in new information the next day. We all know, for example, how a family story gets told each holiday season but, over time, it morphs and changes as important details are forgotten, get left out, or we need our family members to chime in to share their memories of that event. Our brains forget details of stories over time and then we tell new stories at the next family gathering. Old memories get replaced by new memories.

When a memory leaves an emotional imprint and is unprocessed, it does not fade over time and it does not get replaced by newer events. These types of memories do not fade since our bodies cannot afford to forget what happened and what we endured. We cannot take the risk of forgetting what we endured since forgetting may mean that we could be at risk of enduring that same thing repeatedly. Think of the hot stove again. When we think about touching a hot stove, we wince and cringe. Our brain does not forget this pain. Our loved ones can hurt us in the same way. Emotional pain (rejection from a loved one, for instance) hurts in the same ways and places in our brains that physical pain (hot stove) does[5]. For humans, pain registers as pain regardless of the type of pain. Pain creates imprints that inform, shape, and orient us in life. When pain goes unresolved, it scars. Scars toughen tissue and limit our tissue's flexibility. As a result of unprocessed and unresolved pain, we have less emotional flexibility. With scarring, we cannot afford to keep our hearts open. We jump more quickly to negative conclusions (to ensure our survival). **Our responses turn into reactions. Our reactions become habits which harden our hearts, narrow our eyes, and tighten our bodies.**

Exercise 7.1

Losing an important relationship, as you have experienced recently, often leaves an emotional imprint. Not every relationship that ends leaves an imprint, but some lost relationships will leave lots of imprints and scars.

How do I know if I have scarring from the loss of an important relationship? Ask yourself:

- Do I find myself thinking about the events that led to the end of my relationship?
- Do I replay these events again and again?
- Are memories of this person/these events intrusive (uninvited memories that intrude on my experience)?
- Do I have moments of reliving the past?
- Do I have moments of not being able to get the past out of my head?
- Do I have dreams or nightmares about this person or relationship?
- Do I feel haunted by this person?
- Am I pre-occupied by my memories of what happened?
- Am I feeling like I cannot move on?
- Has my past experience with this person limited my current life in any way?
- Has this relationship changed my hopes, dreams, and goals for myself and my future?
- Did the loss of this relationship make me hurt myself or think of harming myself in any way?
- Did the end of this relationship change how I view and think of myself?
- Did the end of this relationship change how I view or think about future love relationships?

Exercise 7.2

If you recognize any of these questions and they resonate with you, let us slow down and take a look at what lingers for you. Write what lingers in your head and heart:

_____

_____

_____

_____

_____

As you are writing what has lingered in your head and heart, notice your body's sensations. Where is there tightness and contraction? Where do you have an interest in avoidance and perhaps denial? What are you feeling as you remind yourself of what you endured and what still lingers? What emotions are coming alive as you think back and put words to your lingering memories:

_____

_____

_____

_____

_____

Remembering your wave style here can really help you to know how to best meet your pain and trauma when it comes alive.

 If you tend to comfortably ride the waves of your emotional pain, then you will meet the challenge of learning from it and growing stronger and wiser as a result. You can practice paying attention to your pain and being with it – tapping into its wisdom. Read on.

 However, if you tend to feel very distant from your pain, you might need to make a special effort to tune into your inner world, to notice signals your body sends that past trauma might be showing up, and to lean into and listen more closely to your inner world.

 If you tend to become rocked by the big waves of your pain, so much that you can become overwhelmed by it, you will need ways to be able to contain it and to gain more of a working distance from your pain as we work through these exercises. This might include dedicated contact-time then taking a break from emotional contact, using a healthy distraction or sharing with another.

 If you tend to become rocked by the big waves of your pain some of the time, and other times find it hard to access or feel your painful emotions, you will need to be aware of which mode you are in. This will help you to become skilled at leaning in when your feelings seem too distant or indistinct and leaning out when they feel too overwhelming. Let us keep going.

Exercise 7.3

Name what hurt you

We would like to start the process of honoring your pain by helping you to name your hurts and to begin to access the pain associated with them. Please be mindful of your wave style as you do this work and be gentle and kind to yourself.

Write some details of your hurts:

_____

_____

_____

_____

_____

Describe what your hurt is like now:

_____

_____

_____

_____

_____

Can you describe a good image for your hurt?

_____

_____

_____

_____

_____

_____

What did this hurt tell you about yourself?

_____

_____

_____

_____

_____

_____

What did this hurt tell you about the other person(s)?

_____

_____

_____

_____

_____

_____

Some people think if we name what hurt us, it will make our hurt and pain worse. They think that naming our hurt will make the pain bigger. These people tell us to "move on" or "forget about it." If only this were possible! The only way to truly move on is to move through the pain, the hurt, and process the memories that grip us. The only way out of the pain is processing through the pain.

How do we process through the pain?

As we start to focus on our pain, it is important to acknowledge that our pain does feel like it gets bigger with our initial focus and attention. This is especially true for pain we have been ignoring, suppressing, or avoiding. As you muster the courage to find your pockets of pain, your focus on these older feelings will make them feel bigger initially. When we focus on a feeling, the attention now on that feeling can make it feel bigger for a few moments. Please know that this initial feeling of the worst pain getting bigger is temporary! When humans feel overwhelmingly uncomfortable feelings getting bigger, most of us flinch and turn away. We say to ourselves that we must find other ways to avoid that feeling because focusing on it did not help at all. This, our friends, is the wrong meaning to make and the wrong message to learn! It is so important to know that when we find our courage to stay with our pain, that initial amplification of the painful feeling does not last!

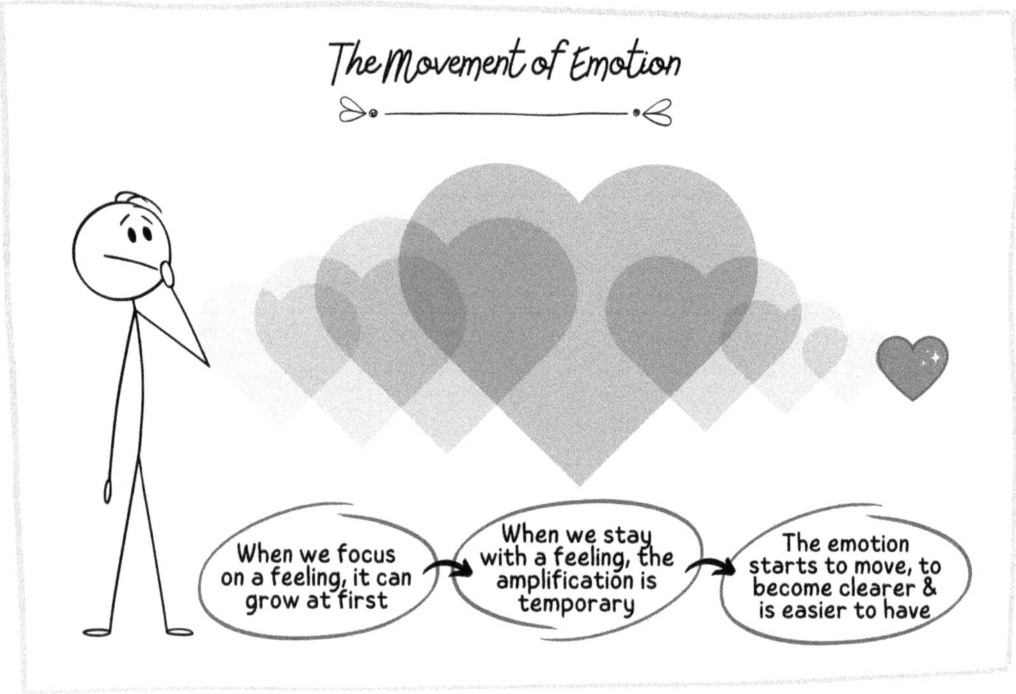

Figure 7.2 The movement of emotion.

As we stay with our pain and breathe through the amplification of it, the emotion starts to move. All emotion has movement in it and most emotion moves like waves. As the painful emotion comes alive and we let it move us, the movement of the emotion starts to contain and shrink the metabolic weight of the emotion. That is right: *the actual movement that emotion needs is the same movement that contains the emotion which makes it feel smaller and more manageable.* As the emotion moves through us, it gets smaller, less chaotic, and more manageable. As a result, we feel less overwhelmed and less flooded by it. As it continues to move inside of us, the waves get smaller and less chaotic. As it continues to move, the pain gets more distilled and organized. As is true for any of our experiences as they become more organized, our emotion too becomes more coherent and cogent. The more coherent it becomes, the easier it is for us to have competence with working with our own emotion. As our competence grows, so too does our confidence in what we are feeling. This is a powerful process of meeting yourself and being with your inner experiences in a way that develops confidence and competence. Our growing confidence informs us and allows us to reference our own emotion again and again as life needs us to! It is hard initially and it feels risky but, pretty quickly, it gets easier and relief is around the corner!

Exercise 7.4

So, how do we heal our emotional injuries, scars, imprints?

A key requirement for healing is safety. Your felt sense of safety. Since safety is the pre-eminent concern of all humans[6], what makes you feel safe is your priority here. Our brains are constantly scanning to ensure our safety and, when we do not feel safe, our brains will remain pre-occupied with our lack of safety until we can establish our safety. Establishing safety for yourself is your next task.

Let us start by highlighting the role of your physical safety in your environment. Not all environments lead to us feeling safe. Some key elements of safety in your physical environment are your physical comfort, assurance of privacy, and having the ability to attend to your biological needs (food, water, restroom, etc.).

What are some of the qualities you need to feel safe in your physical environment?

_____

_____

_____

_____

_____

The next level of safety we want to orient you toward is your emotional safety. Emotional safety is the sense that you are safe to be who you are. You can be yourself, especially in front of others. Emotional safety derives from safe social connections. Neurologically speaking, we get our emotional safety from our interactions with important others and receiving cues of safety from these important others. Name those in your life that you have some emotional safety with (it is okay to name your therapist, if you have one):

_____

_____

_____

_____

_____

_____

The next step of the process is to name your triggers. Present moment situations and experiences that bring us back to our moments of most intense fear, panic or aloneness are called "triggers." Some researchers describe triggers as moments when an emotional state "hijacks" your brain. Triggers can be people, places, events, sounds, smells, anything that resembles or brings the traumatic event back into the present moment and make us feel like it (the traumatic event) is happening again. We all feel scared and out of control at these moments. The very nature of triggers is that we can perceive the current situation to be as real as the past situation, whether it is or is not. Real or perceived, our bodies respond to triggers as if the same scary event is happening again. One recent example: a man who was falsely accused and spent twenty years in prison for a crime he did not commit came home (finally!). His family always used a certain brand of soap. Unexpectedly, his partner brought home a new soap and this good man was triggered by its smell. Without knowing, his partner brought home the only soap this man had access to for twenty years in prison (for a crime he did not commit) and the smell of it triggered him into panic and rage. This triggering event scared him and his family. His rage was so big. Nobody understood it. The strength of it was overwhelming and it took a few hours for the trigger to calm a bit. As his panic and rage settled, a few days later, he and his partner were brave enough to talk about it. Thankfully, he could name his trigger (the smell of prison soap). Suddenly, his unexpected reaction made perfect sense to his partner and then to his family members. He was able to talk about how the trigger happened for him. As he allowed himself to observe his emotional world and talked it through in this way, he became predictable to himself and his family again. And, thankfully, as part of the repair process, he was able to hear how his triggered-state scared his loved ones. Now, he and his partner are learning to cope with triggers together and his adult children can be aware of his triggers and be protective when needed. He now has his own support and that of his family. He is no longer alone with this pain. It is hard enough that triggers are often unpredictable (until we make them known to ourselves and our loved ones). Once triggered, we also become unpredictable to ourselves and our loved ones. The unpredictability takes a toll. Becoming predictable again is an important component to restore balance and connection after a trigger both with yourself and your loved ones.

When you think back to your most intense moments of fear and aloneness, what triggers you into that panic state (name your triggers)?

_____

_____

_____

_____

_____

_____

When a trigger happens, how does your body respond?

_____

_____

_____

_____

_____

_____

After your body responds, you get yourself to a safe place, then what do you feel?

_____

_____

_____

_____

_____

_____

Can you share what happened – I got triggered – with a safe other? If so, with whom can you share?

_____

_____

_____

_____

_____

_____

Faulty alarm system

Many of us who have endured more than most develop what one researcher calls a "faulty alarm system"[7]. As a result of enduring, trauma survivors react more quickly, make more negative meaning and do not have the joy of being curious which, at times, means we are reacting as if there is a "faulty alarm" signaling danger. You too would react more quickly and negatively if you had been overwhelmed and left alone by trauma! Our nervous system is wired into us to keep us safe, but can become a broken or faulty alarm system as a result of trauma. In order to ensure our survival, we will jump up and run at the smell of smoke, metaphorically-speaking, before we realize it is just a burnt piece of toast. This is a simple example of how trauma always rewires our nervous systems in service of our survival. Trauma survivors do not have the luxury of wondering if it is toast burning or if the house is on fire. Their nervous systems cannot afford to take that moment to pause, to wonder, and to investigate. Instead, their wiring throws them into reacting as if there is a catastrophe happening. This is not their fault. Trauma survivors have earned their defenses. These defenses have saved their lives a hundred times already.

While being on the lookout for threat keeps you safe, it is also exhausting. As humans, our nervous systems are wired to scan for threat, but we actually need connection with others to turn off our threat perception. Stephen Porges[8] describes that we cope with threat and function at our best when our Social Engagement System (SES) is activated. Social Engagement means connecting with others and this is the highest priority for the human nervous system. Safe relationships are our first lines of defense – our best form of protection – and are required for us to flourish as humans. We all get our safety from being in healthy relationships. In fact, it is pretty difficult to rest and recuperate without safe connection with others. The science is really clear about this these days. In healthy relationships, our loved ones naturally use their facial expressions, voice tones, and gestures to send signals of safety to us. Our nervous system is highly attuned to these safety signals and is always on the lookout for them. This is love in action and these three elements – facial expressions, tone of voice, and gestures – are how we convey safety to all we care about.

So, as you are learning, our individual safety is a relationship task. *Feeling safe comes from within our relationships.* When past relationships were not safe or did not provide protection for us, our nervous systems were rewired so that we could provide our own protection. This was not a choice. This happened within us as needed over time. Stephen Porges has a term called, "neuroception."[9] Below and behind our awareness, our nervous systems are constantly evaluating our environment – especially our

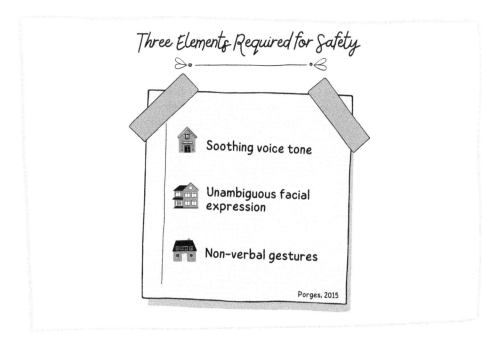

Figure 7.3 Three elements required for safety.

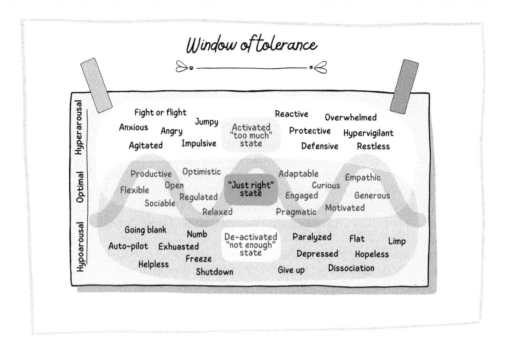

Figure 7.4 Window of tolerance.

relationships – to ensure our safety. Since our brains are vigilant to threat, the more we have endured and the more alone we are, the more watchful and wary our brains become and remain. When we have endured more than most and no repair is provided, our neuroception re-sets in the service of our own protection. As a result of this re-set, we react more quickly and make more negative meaning about situations to get us ready to defend – whether we need to or not. Again, real or perceived, we get ready to defend because nature favors false positives over false negatives every day of the week! Our brains and bodies would much prefer to be prepared to defend without needing to than to be unprepared to defend in the face of a real threat. Because of this, we stay guarded. We stay defensive. We regularly perceive danger or threat even if not there. As the saying goes, "better to be safe than sorry!"

Unfortunately, when we are tuned to possible threat in this way, we will have bigger reactions than expected. This is hard for us and this is hard for our loved ones. We have bigger reactions to ensure we take appropriate actions when our survival is at stake (even if only figuratively). We do not get to make a cognitive choice about whether or not our survival is in jeopardy. For all of us, it is a visceral experience and an immediate reaction. The hard part is that we do not often know the reality of our survival being at risk until after the threatening event is over. It is only when looking back at the event or the fright that we can gauge if our survival was literally at risk or if we were overreacting.

Another way to describe triggers is by thinking about what happens in our bodies when we are triggered. Essentially, a trigger is anything that pushes us outside of our emotional Window of Tolerance.[10] Our Window of Tolerance is our emotional comfort zone. We all have a zone where we are most comfortable emotionally. When triggered, we are instantly out of our comfort zone and that explains we have reactions (instead of responses).

Exercise 7.5

If you relate to this or if this resonates with you in any way, spend a few minutes thinking back on recent events when you had a big reaction. Remember, your big reactions are real, justified, and needed. You are not wrong to have big reactions. They are happening in service of your protection, safety, and survival. Your past has informed your nervous system how best to protect you, so there is nothing wrong with any of your reactions. As you heal, though, we want to help you sensitize yourself to those moments of big reaction, overreaction or having a faulty alarm system response mostly because these moments are hard on you and your loved ones. Essentially, it is a stress response that wears you down and takes precious time and energy to recover from. If we can help you work with your moments of big reactions, then your reactions will start to become responses. Responses are much less stressful on your body and your loved ones than reactions!

When you look back, when was a recent time you had an overreaction in response to a trigger?

_____

_____

_____

_____

_____

_____

Write how you saw yourself cope. What were your behaviors?

_____

_____

_____

_____

_____

_____

What do you remember feeling then? What do you feel now remembering this event?

_____

_____

_____

_____

_____

_____

Can you share about this with a safe other? If so, with whom can you share this?

_____

_____

_____

_____

_____

_____

Finding the order in experience

The entire reason for tracking our own triggers and how we cope with them (behaviorally and emotionally) is so that we can process our fight, flight, or freeze responses. Triggers are uncomfortable, intense, scary, difficult to manage, and demand our full attention. As we grab hold of our triggers and process the emotions that are embedded in them and occur as a result of them, you are going to be able to stay more present in these types of distressing moments. All emotions embedded in our triggers are chaotic in nature. As emotions emerge, the chaos intensifies. When we can stay with the intense waves of emotion, however, the chaos shifts into some coherence. Pieces of your emotion will start making more and more sense. This growing emotional coherence will feel more settling on the inside of you. As your emotions become more settled, you will naturally start feeling more emotionally competent and confident. Your emotional reactions will be less overwhelming and more familiar. As with any process, the more familiar you are with it, the easier it is to manage and your confidence will continue to grow. You will have fewer triggering events and when they happen, your reactions will be less intense.

The healing of trauma comes when we can stay in the present moment experience without going back to the traumatic event. You will start having a different experience of the past moments that have been triggering. Having a different experience in the present moment again and again is how we neutralize the potency of past trauma. As you relate more and more with your triggers, you will start to be able to shift into observing your triggers. Observing your triggers is so different from becoming gripped, overwhelmed, and flooded by them.

Our hope for you and what we have been working toward in this session is your growing abilities to stay with yourself in real time and to use your inner world as a reference for strength and reassurance – even while uncomfortable. As you have focused again and again on your emotions and your inner world, you have become more and more familiar with your emotions and your ways of coping. As you have become more and more familiar, your competency with your inner world has grown, as has your confidence! Regularly referencing your body and emotions empowers you to know exactly how you are feeling and coping moment-to-moment. This kind of self-awareness takes the mystery out of the world of emotions and coping strategies and gives you the key to riding the waves of your inner world without feeling like you will drown!

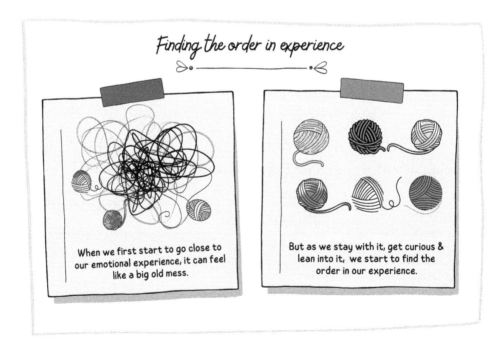

Figure 7.5 Finding the order in experience.

Notes

1 Junger, S. (2015). How PTSD became a problem far beyond the battlefield. *Vanity Fair*, June.
2 Levine, P. (2017). Featured expert. *National Institute for the Clinical Application of Behavioral Medicine (NICABM)*. Online.
3 Olden, J. (2018). Presentation in *The EFT Cafe*. Online.
4 Lewis, T., Amini, F. & Lannon, R. (2000). *A General Theory of Love*. Vintage Books: New York.
5 Feeney, J. (2009). When love hurts: Understanding hurtful events in couple relationships. In Vangelisti (Ed.) *Feeling Hurt in Close Relationships*, pp. 313–335. Cambridge: Cambridge University Press.
6 de Becker, G. (1997). *The Gift of Fear: Survival Signals that Protect Us from Violence*. New York: Little, Brown and Company.
7 van der Kolk, B. (2014). *The Body Keeps the Score: Brain, Mind, and Body in the Healing of Trauma*. New York: Penguin Press.
8 Porges, S. (2011). *The Polyvagal Theory: Neurophysiological Foundations of Emotions, Attachment, Communications, and Self-regulation*. New York: W.W. Norton & Company.
9 Porges, S. (2011). *The Polyvagal Theory: Neurophysiological Foundations of Emotions, Attachment, Communications, and Self-regulation*. New York: W.W. Norton & Company.
10 Siegel, D. J. (1999). *The Developing Mind*. New York: Guilford Press.

Processing the enormity of grief and loss

In this session we dive deeply into the grief of loss. We will be naming, owning, and making room for the ruthless pain that accompanies the loss of an important relationship. We will explore and process the big, painful feelings that might be there for you, and will find what you need at your core to help you in your adjustment to this loss. This involves not only acknowledging the loss of someone special and all that this relationship could have been (this is extremely difficult for many), but also acknowledging the things that might have been missing for you, your unmet attachment needs (also very difficult). We will find a pathway into and through the grief and look at how to be sure that you are grieving in healthy ways, ways that allow you to process this loss and move forward stronger for it.

In his model of separation and loss, John Bowlby described our predictable reactions to loss as: numbing, yearning and searching (protest), disorganization and despair, and reorganization and detachment[1]. In this session, we will focus on the disorganization and despair phase of this important process. We will explore what it means to confront the reality of the loss, to give up searching and fighting to recover the bond, and to plunge headlong into the despair of knowing it cannot be recovered, that it is forever altered. This is harrowing and painful work, but confronting this loss and allowing yourself to process these big emotions is all part of the work of grief.

Exercise 8.1

Let's start this process by naming and acknowledging the loss you have experienced. You have lost someone extremely special to you, and in losing or redefining this relationship, you have lost not only this person, but all you shared together and all you planned to share for the future.

Remember, it hurts because it matters, and your pain honors the love you felt, and indeed may still feel, for this special person. If you are willing to open your heart to love, then you risk bravely. Your risk has left you hurt this time, but it won't always hurt this much, and you will find love again – but first, we need to help your poor, sore heart to heal.
Can you name this loss?

"I have lost my relationship as I knew it with_____ and this hurts terribly."

Can you read that again and feel into it? Take a few deep breaths and allow the feeling to emerge, to grow, and to be felt. Breathe into it and allow it to be here. Just know that being with this pain will allow you to process it, hang in there with us.

As you allow yourself to feel this loss, to let it be there, what shows up for you right now?

Feelings:

_____

_____

_____

_____

DOI: 10.4324/9781003360506-11

Sensations:

_____

_____

_____

_____

Thoughts:

_____

_____

_____

_____

Images:

_____

_____

_____

_____

Exercise 8.2

Grief from the loss of a relationship often has layers of emotion that accompany the understandable sadness that loss brings with it. If your partner lives on but no longer chooses you, the combination of loss and rejection can be unbearable. If you have made the gut-wrenching decision to end a relationship, knowing that you are inflicting pain on someone you care about, this is a painful mix of guilt *and* loss. Even when both partners make a mutual decision to end or redefine their relationship, despite trying really hard to make it work, the pain and helplessness can be overwhelming. When a bond is snapped beyond repair by an act of betrayal, then the loss is compounded by broken promises and agonizing hurt. If you are the one who broke the trust, then the self-reproach in combination with the loss can be monumental. Whichever way you have come upon your loss and pain, we know that it will be creating its own brand of suffering – we need to make space for this to be heard, acknowledged, and learned from.

Do you notice more feelings or sensations arrive as you touch this loss such as anger, hurt, regret, guilt, shame, fear? Note these here:

_____

_____

_____

_____

_____

_____

_____

As you notice the emotions that are evoked by thinking about your loss, pay attention to what you tend to do with those feelings. Do you tend to push them aside? Do they stop you in your tracks?

What do you typically do when these feelings show up?

_____

_____

_____

_____

How does this impact your feelings? Does it make them easier to have or more difficult to have? Does it make it easier or harder to go about your life?

_____

_____

_____

_____

Which wave style fits best to describe how you tend to experience your feelings of grief and loss for this lost relationship?

| Big Waves | Distant Waves | Hybrid Waves | Riding the Waves |

Figure 8.1 Circle the "wave style" that best fits you. Look out for this icon next to exercises best suited to this style of expressing and experiencing emotion.

Take a note of this, we are going to come back to it.

Turning your world upside down

While we will usually fight to keep our attachment bonds and protest their loss strenuously, when a human accepts the brutal realization that someone special to them is lost to them, most are expected to collapse into sadness. In this phase of recovery, the true reality of the loss is encountered, hope recedes, and a person's world is turned upside down.

The loss of our safe haven of comfort and secure base of support is devastating. It is no wonder that once we accept that no amount of protesting will bring our special other back and we can accept the reality of the loss, it is disorganizing for us. Not only is loss emotionally painful, it turns our world upside down. You are not just grieving the loss of your special person; you are grieving the lost fabric of your life.

The way in which you arrived at your loss will play a role in the disorganizing impact it is likely to have for you. For instance, if you were blindsided by this loss, if your trust was betrayed, if you did things you were not proud of, then you are likely to be questioning who your partner is, who you are, and where your life is going. There is likely to be a stronger feeling of disorganization for you. If your relationship ended slowly over time, if there was a sense of warning for its demise, then your life might feel less upended than for sudden, unexpected losses. Despite this, loss is loss and change is difficult. And this is not just any change, the loss of an attachment figure is an enormous thing for us humans.

Exercise 8.3

You have taken the brave step of allowing yourself to feel the pain of this loss. Now, let us make room for the utter disorganization that comes with accepting a loss of this magnitude.

How has this loss made you question yourself, the other, the past, the future?

_____

_____

_____

_____

_____

_____

_____

_____

_____

What is hardest for you to understand or to reconcile?

_____

_____

_____

_____

What unanswered questions linger for you?

_____

_____

_____

_____

_____

How do you manage this confusion?

_____

_____

_____

_____

_____

How do you feel as you allow yourself to connect with these questions?

_____

_____

_____

_____

What is healthy grief?

Relationship loss shares a common set of challenges, and these are *interpersonal*, as in how you negotiate your ongoing relationship with your ex-partner and your life without them, and *intrapersonal*, as in how you manage the grief and loss within yourself. "Successful grief" means that you can accept and adapt to the loss of someone special so that you might be able to move on with your life, perhaps even stronger for the experience of that connection.

The researchers who study the process of grief and loss generally reject the idea of grief being a linear process, preferring to see the process of grief as involving four key tasks. This is an empowering and active view of grief that appreciates that the griever can achieve these four tasks:

1. Acceptance of the reality of the loss.
2. Experiencing the pain of the loss.

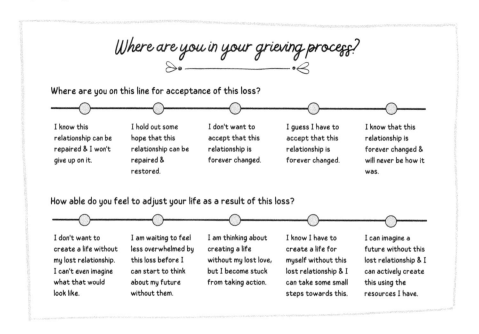

Figure 8.2 Where are you in your grieving process?

3. Adjusting to life without the lost love.
4. Finding a connection to the past without becoming stuck in it[2].

Grieving is an emotional and organic process that evolves and shifts. People's experience of grief will vary greatly in terms of how they might approach these tasks. You may experience periods of animated protest against the separation and make attempts to contact your ex-partner for resolution and then sink into despair at other moments, crying and unmotivated to face the world. You will have good days where you can attend to the functional aspects of life and glimpse some hope for the future, and you will have bad days where you are consumed with the injustice or the despair of the loss and wonder how you will ever go on. Overall, the hope is that you will gradually move *forward* as you process your feelings and make sense of the loss.

Approaching the "work" of grief

Let's look at how you can attend to the "work" of grieving in the most healthy and adaptive way possible. Of course, we always recommend being gentle with yourself and respecting your own emotional process. Our aim is to give you a guide to follow so that you can respectfully shape your grieving process in a way that will take you into and through it. So that you might be able to use this loss for growth.

Coping with a loss of this magnitude involves two important emotional processes at once, turning up the heat in some areas, and turning down the heat in others. To illustrate this, it helps to think of the "work" of grief as involving two important areas of focus[3]. The first is the *emotional* work of processing the loss. This includes, thinking about the lost partner, yearning for them, reflecting on the relationship and how it ended, remembering the good times, and learning from the not-so-good times, and being with the pain of the loss. Emotional work of this nature is taxing, and no-one can do this exclusively. People need to be able to come up for air or they would become overwhelmed by their emotional pain, and they would not be able to function.

The other equally important focus of grieving is the *practical* work of coping with day-to-day life and adjusting the practical aspects of your life to the loss. This might involve making decisions about living arrangements, changes to finances, managing co-parenting of any children, changing employment status, or the building of new social connections. As you can see, this is quite a distinct process compared to the emotional work of processing the loss, but that does not mean that there is not an emotional element to these life decisions and adjustments.

In this way, both the emotional and the practical tasks of grieving are equally important to a person's progress in adjusting to the separation from their special person. Healthy grief is thought to balance these two tasks and to move flexibly between them so that emotions can be attended to, and life-transitioning can be accomplished.

Exercise 8.4

As you reflect on these two tasks, the emotional and the practical, which do you find yourself naturally doing more of? Why might that be?

_____

_____

_____

_____

_____

_____

Which task seems more difficult for you to attend to? Why might that be?

_____

_____

_____

_____

_____

Keep this in mind. We are going to come back to this too!

How does your attachment/coping strategy impact how you grieve?

We suspect that you will be unsurprised by this point to hear that a person's attachment strategy impacts not just how they navigate close relationships with others but also how they process loss and grief.

 Research has shown that people with a secure attachment strategy (riding the waves) are more likely to regulate their emotions, to seek support from others, and to move more smoothly through the process of grieving a lost relationship than those who use insecure attachment strategies (anxious, avoidant, or hybrid).

 People with an *anxious* attachment strategy (big waves) are more likely to be tuned into their partner's availability and to be sensitive to cues of possible rejection, so the loss of an attachment figure is extremely distressing. Following the end of a relationship, people with an anxious attachment strategy are more likely to become preoccupied with thoughts of their ex-partner, to make attempts to repair or reconcile and to continue to seek-out their ex-partner as a source of support. These tendencies can play a role in slowing the adjustment process.

 People who use an *avoidant* attachment strategy (distant waves) might be more at risk of speeding through the grieving process and not processing the loss enough. This might be because an avoidant attachment strategy often involves emotional distancing from themselves and their partner, and so they might not form as deep an emotional connection, which could leave them either less emotionally impacted by their loss or less aware of the emotional impact of the loss on their emotional world[4].

 The research on the impact of attachment strategies on post-relationship adjustment seems to be limited to looking at secure, anxious, and avoidant attachment strategies. The hybrid (fearful-avoidant) attachment strategy is not exclusively explored, possibly because this attachment strategy incorporates features of anxious pursuit for connection *and* avoidant withdrawal from closeness. Despite this, we can expect that in grief and loss, people with a hybrid attachment strategy might experience both anxious distress at the loss and withdrawal from the ex-partner in oscillating amounts. If you identify with this attachment strategy, take a moment to notice which mode (as in anxious pursuit – big waves, or avoidance – distant waves) might be more dominant for you in your grieving.

Exercise 8.5

Thinking back to the first exercise in this session, when you allowed yourself to feel the emotions related to this loss, which wave style best described how you experience your emotions in relation to this loss (circle)?

I experience my emotions as huge waves that I feel intensely. They can be all-consuming and I can find it difficult to focus on the practical tasks of life when they show up.

I am quite removed from my emotions in relation to this loss. I am aware of them, but they are quite distant. I try to not think about the loss too much, preferring to focus on the task at hand.

At times, I can become overwhelmed by the intensity of my emotions in relation to this loss and at other times, I can feel removed from them. It can be difficult to know which strategy (avoidant or anxious) I might be using at any given time.

I am aware of my painful feelings when they show up and can let myself feel them deeply. I can also gain enough distance from them to focus on other things when I need to.

By now, we anticipate that you will be aware of the similarity between how you experience your emotions in relation to this loss and your general attachment/coping strategy. This makes sense and reflects how your closest relationships early in life taught you powerful lessons about how to navigate close relationships – with others *and* with yourself.

Your attachment or coping strategy will naturally impact which task of grief you find easier and which you find more difficult. For instance, those with an anxious attachment strategy will be more likely to experience their emotions as big, all-consuming waves that can make it difficult to attend to the practical adjustments that need to happen as part of processing this loss. Those with an avoidant attachment strategy will be more likely to experience their emotions as distant waves and therefore, they might find the practical tasks easy, but could miss out on an opportunity for growth that can come from the emotional work of grieving.

Reflecting back on the previous exercises and noting which of the tasks of grief come more easily to you, tick which applies to you:

Emotional tasks of grieving:

- I can allow myself to feel my emotions about this loss.
- I can sometimes become overwhelmed by my feelings.
- I think about my lost love and where it went wrong.
- I can remember the good times we shared.
- I get sad when I think about what we had.
- I grieve for the future we were going to share.
- I tell others about my feelings and seek their support.
- Add your own:

_____

_____

_____

_____

Practical tasks of grieving:

- I can put my pain aside to get on with my responsibilities.
- I can make the changes I need to make now that my person is no longer in my life.
- I try not to let myself feel my pain too much.
- I distract myself with positive or mundane tasks.
- I can reorganize my life to take into account the absence of the other.
- I can rely on myself to cope.
- I do not share my feelings with others.

- Add your own:

_____

_____

_____

_____

Notice which category has more ticks. The one with the least ticks might need some more of your attention to make sure that you are achieving a balanced approach to your grieving.

Achieving healthy grief

It is important that you keep an eye on *both* the emotional and the practical tasks of grieving so that neither area is neglected. We know that becoming engulfed in waves of painful emotion for extended periods of time is going to impact a person's ability to function in life and we know that suppressing painful emotions is effortful and wearing on a person's wellbeing[5]. So long as you can pay attention to whether you might experience a reluctance in either task and intentionally tune into it, then you are flexibly meeting the challenge of grief. You could call this "Goldilocks flexibility."

For instance, someone with avoidant attachment strategies might naturally find themselves turning to the practical tasks of making life-adjustments and moving away from the emotional tasks required to process the loss. They might need to lean into their emotional processing of the loss and really tune into their sad feelings to be sure that they are honored. Someone with anxious attachment strategies might naturally do the emotional work of grieving but feel out of their depth in navigating the practical adjustments they need to make to move forwards from the loss. They might need to work to create more distance from their emotional reactions and to allocate some time for focusing on the practical arrangements that need to be made to ready themselves for the next phase of their life.

Exercise 8.6

Which of the two tasks of grief (emotional or practical) do I need to actively build?

_____

_____

_____

_____

_____ For those who need to tune into the waves of their emotional world to attend to the emotional
≈≈≈ work of grief, here are some ideas (tick which ones appeal to you):

- Create a reminder to regularly check-in on how you are feeling throughout the day – name the feeling and notice the sensations and thoughts that come with it.
- Make time to think about your lost love and to let yourself feel the pain of the loss.
- Journal about the loss or write an unsent letter to your ex-partner.
- Reflect on the positive things you learned from this relationship.
- Reflect on the things you are sad to lose.
- Ask yourself what you would have done differently if you had known more.
- Connect with what you are most longing for in your closest relationships.
- Think about how you could signal your needs to those who matter most.

For those who tend to experience their emotions as too intense to be able to attend to the practical work of grief, here are some ideas (tick which ones appeal to you):

- Make time to think about your lost love each day but set a time limit on this and do something positive, restorative, or distracting at the end of this time.
- Write down your thoughts so that they are not free-floating and then actively engage in another activity.
- Use mindfulness, meditation, or relaxation practices.
- Make a list of distracting activities that you can call on when you need a break.
- Move your body.
- Reach out to others for support (not your ex-partner).
- Get help with managing the practical life-adjustments you need to make.
- Set yourself small goals to make the practical changes you need to make and commit to working on them each day in some small way.

 For those who use both anxious and avoidant strategies (hybrid), it might help to select items from each of the above lists to use when you notice yourself either staying distant from your emotional pain or being engulfed by it.

When processing your grief and balancing the emotional and practical tasks of grief, it is important to keep within a workable window of tolerance[6] (remember this from last session). This window needs to be open wide enough that you are able to make contact with your painful feelings in order to process the loss adaptively. This means being able to engage with your experience, to tune into your needs, and best figure out how to move forward – all informed by the wisdom of your emotional world. However, the window needs to not be so wide that all feelings engulf you and throw you off balance – reeling into old ways of coping that you know are not good for you. And, conversely, this window needs to not be so narrow that you get more and more distant from the very emotion that gives your life color, meaning, and purpose. Remember, "Goldilocks flexibility." This is somewhat of an art form.

Above all, if you are processing emotion, focusing on practicalities, and allowing yourself to breathe, then no matter how messy and disorganized it might appear, you are doing the work needed to successfully navigate this loss.

Exercise 8.7

Note down 4 things that you can do to make sure that you are attending to the work of grief that fits best for you:

1. _____

2. _____

3. _____

4. _____

Note down 4 resources you have to help you along this path (people, places, things):

1. _____

2. _____

3. _____

4. _____

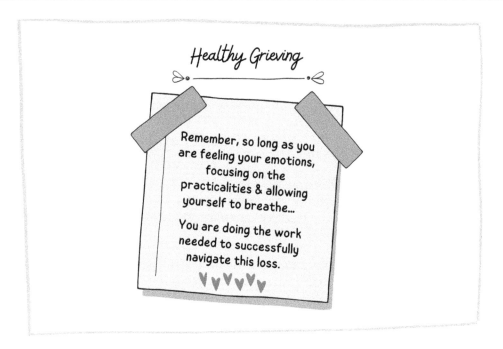

Figure 8.3 Reminders for healthy grieving.

Note down 2 sustaining things you can say to yourself as you do this difficult work:

1. _____

2. _____

As this session comes to a close, so too does Part Two of this workbook. You have gone deeper and completed a lot of really important, essential, and substantial work in Part Two. You walked through the process of facing your fears (Session Five). You learned the whys and the hows of riding the waves of your anger in Session Six. In Session Seven, you were so brave in focusing on naming and healing your emotional scars. As we wrap up this session, your courage and bravery continued as you processed your grief and loss, which is monumental. It is no easy feat to turn toward and make sense of the impacts of grief and loss. But, as you know so well at this point, much better to have turned toward your grief, loss, and pain than to have tried to find additional ways to suppress and avoid since suppression and avoidance never work long-term. You have been strong. You are strong and you are growing your resilience session by session!

Notes

1 Bowlby, J. (1979). *The Making and Breaking of Affectional Bonds*. London: Tavistock.
2 Worden, W. J. (2018). *Grief Counseling and Grief Therapy, 5th Edition: A Handbook for the Mental Health Professional*. New York: Springer Publishing Company.
3 Stroebe, M. & Schut, H. (1999). The dual process model of coping with bereavement: Rationale and description. *Death Studies*, 23, 197–224.
4 Davis, D., Shaver, P. R. & Vernon, M. L. (2003). Physical, emotional and behavioral reactions to breaking up: The roles of gender, age, emotional involvement, and attachment style. *Personality & Social Psychology Bulletin*, 29 (7), 871–884.
5 Gross, J. J. & Levenson, R. W. (1997). Hiding feelings: The acute effects of inhibited negative and positive emotion. *Journal of Abnormal Psychology*, 106 (1), 95–103.
6 Siegel, D. J. (1999). *The Developing Mind*. New York: Guilford Press.

Part III

Growing Momentum

Forgiving and letting go

Welcome to Part Three, the final part of this session-by-session journey you have embarked on. In this session, Session Nine, we focus on letting go. This means finding meaning from the pain, regret, guilt, fear, and sadness, and fully letting go. We want this for you so that you can move forward in your life – open to all possibilities and limited by none. We want to help you to forgive yourself and others, where needed, and to reconcile what has happened in a way that builds your resilience. Growing from suffering does not take away the pain or mean that you have to be grateful for what has happened (far from it), but that the two states of pain and growth can and do co-exist.

When we suffer, as you have, it is only natural that you would want to find meaning in that suffering. We are here to help you to find the meaning in this experience so that it can be a source of personal growth. Our wish is that this will allow you to move forward in your life, with greater self-awareness, self-compassion, and connection with yourself. You will find that you can be healed and whole again. Your survival narrative will be beautiful and powerful. And we will be cheering you on every step of the way. So let us get started!

The opportunity in suffering

We know that the loss of a relationship is among the highest-rated stressful events that we can encounter as humans. In an ideal world, you can learn from this painful event so that it can be a source of personal growth. The idea that good can come from hardship is age-old, and we think this represents the remarkable human capacity to adapt, respond, and thrive. That does not mean that it is *easy*, but the most important lessons never are, unfortunately. However, humans facing difficult situations are capable of positive change, of not just surviving a difficult experience and returning to normal functioning, but of growing *beyond* their normal functioning. This is the concept of post-traumatic growth[1]. This is what we want for you!

Exercise 9.1

We do not grow if the lesson does not fully grab our attention. Your pain is taking you somewhere important. In fact, an essential element that determines if a person experiences growth from a trauma is how disorganizing it is to their inner world. This bears repeating: *the more disorganizing the experience has been for you, the more growth is possible!* When something goes wrong in your life, so wrong that it challenges all your assumptions about the world, about right and wrong, good and bad, about the order of things, about your place in the world, then it is powerful enough to change your view of everything.

Throughout your work in this book so far what have you come to learn about:

Your unmet needs in your past relationship(s)?

_____

_____

_____

_____

_____

DOI: 10.4324/9781003360506-13

Your contribution to the disconnection in your last relationship (i.e. how did you signal your needs and how did this contribute to a negative cycle?):

_____

_____

_____

_____

_____

What have you come to learn about your own attachment strategy (i.e. what your attachment or coping strategy looks like and whether it helps or hinders your needs being met in relationships)?

_____

_____

_____

_____

_____

How are you now interacting differently with your emotional world after working through the exercises in this book?

_____

_____

_____

_____

_____

This information represents powerful learning! These reflections and lessons will be with you and will be carried with you into all your future relationships.

Where there is pain of this type, there is the opportunity for this to transform into a resource for growth and meaning. It is not enough to have just faced hardship. Transformation happens as a result of *how* a person faces that hardship. We put the pain to good use by being willing to examine the shattered expectations and assumptions, by being willing to feel the big feelings, and by taking action that helps you to adjust and revise your life. This means accepting the loss and stepping out of destructive patterns that keep you stuck in experiencing your emotions "too much" or "not enough" as we have looked at in previous sessions.

Exercise 9.2

We can find meaning in the most harrowing of experiences. Some of the benefits of post-traumatic growth are:

- Increased appreciation of life.
- Realigning of priorities.
- Closer and more meaningful relationships with others.
- Increased empathy and compassion for others.

- Increased awareness of your own personal strength.
- Tuning into your spirituality.
- Forging a new direction in life[2].

Now that is awe-inspiring adaptation in action!

In reading the list above, tick the opportunities for growth that you have become aware of from this harrowing life event. Can you share with us more about these below?

_____

_____

_____

_____

_____

_____

_____

_____

What have you learned about yourself that has surprised you?

_____

_____

_____

_____

_____

_____

_____

How has this loss shaped or changed your view of what you want for the future?

_____

_____

_____

_____

_____

_____

_____

These positive changes reflect an ongoing life-long process of the development of wisdom. They represent a happy by-product of adversity; of not merely surviving, but flourishing.

Exercise 9.3

As we have emphasized, *how* you engage with your inner world in the processing of a negative event determines whether you become stuck and dwell on the negative aspects in a ruminative way, or whether you process and move through the pain to a place of reorganization. The meaning we make from our experiences is so important in whether we remain stuck in old self-defeating patterns, or whether we can break out of them and forge new patterns moving forward. Finding a way to honor your emotional experience, and not become swallowed up by unhelpful themes seems to be a delicate balance.

The exercises in this book are designed to help you to be with your inner world in such a way that you can honor your emotional process and access your deepest needs and values. As you well know by now, we advocate *being with* your emotional experiences to tap into the wisdom embedded in those experiences. This means hanging out with your feelings!

We want to offer a word of caution though: there is a difference between wallowing and immersing. Wallowing is a *helpless* process that has the risk of being pulled under, whereas immersing is a *conscious act of being with* your experience to learn from it and to grow.

Immersing is intentional and deliberate, while wallowing is not. Immersing means moving *into* and *through* your emotional experience where wallowing can be a sign of becoming *stuck* in your experience.

Danger zone: I know that I am "wallowing" in unhelpful themes and negative spirals when I start telling myself:

_____

_____

_____

_____

_____

_____

Growth zone: When I am "immersing" myself in my emotional world and listening to my deepest needs and longings this is what I tend to hear:

_____

_____

_____

_____

_____

_____

If this is difficult to do, an example might be *"I hear that I am a good person who makes mistakes but who is learning and growing. I now know that I deserve love, that I am worthy of my needs. I now know that I can ask for them from the people who matter most to me, and that I can be there for myself in new ways."*

Redefining the other

Part of the work to reorganize the inner structures, tendencies, and expectations you hold, is to shift your natural need to reach out to your ex-partner as a source of co-regulation in times of need. To break the pattern of turning to your ex-partner for your felt sense of security can be difficult, but break it you must, in order for you to fully detach. This requires you to redefine the other person in your mind as no longer part of your "inner circle" of special attachment figures. They are no longer able to be accessible to you, responsive to your needs or engaged with you on an emotional level. They cannot be your safe haven or secure base. While they might remain in your life in some way, your bond needs to be "undone" and renegotiated so as to release you both from your close emotional tie.

Exercise 9.4

How does this feel for you to accept that your lost love can no longer be an attachment figure for you? Is this easy or difficult to accept? What feelings show up?

_____

_____

_____

_____

_____

_____

How could you redirect your attachment needs (e.g. support, encouragement, comfort, belonging) to others?

_____

_____

_____

_____

_____

_____

Can you make a commitment to build some attachment relationships, to reduce contact with those who do not hold your best interest at heart and to expand your circle of attachment figures in your world? Write that down here:

_____

_____

_____

_____

_____

_____

Letting go

An important part of the reorganization of your inner world and detachment from a close relationship is making sense of the loss and achieving distance from the intensity of the emotional fall-out. This is especially difficult if you have been wronged by your ex-partner and have not felt heard, or if your hurt has not been acknowledged. When someone we loved and trusted hurts us or rejects us, we tend to feel pain, hostility, and anger, which can translate into unhelpful behaviors. We can become caught in destructive patterns of avoidance or aggressive pursuit in an attempt for some relief from this hurt. When this anger is directed at ourselves then this is especially difficult to resolve. While this is a *protective* coping strategy designed to keep us safe, it can lead us into unproductive behaviors that keep us dwelling on hurts that cannot be resolved, and this can actually reinforce our distress. Forgiveness, as part of your recovery from loss and hurt, can be an important part of the process.

How easily you can achieve forgiveness depends on many factors related to the relationship, the nature of the hurt, your experiences with previous hurts and much more. However, your *attachment strategy* can also play a role.

 Research has shown us that those with a secure attachment strategy (riding the waves) find it easier to forgive transgressions because they tend to hold more positive views of others and to interpret their behavior more benignly. They are also more likely to use effective emotional regulation strategies and to turn to others for support in times of distress[3].

 People with an anxious attachment strategy (big waves) tend to struggle more with forgiveness. This is because they are more likely to dwell on these hurts and to attribute negative meaning to the other's actions.[4] This leaves very little room for processing this hurt in a new light. In addition to this, people with an anxious attachment strategy are likely to keep reaching out to their ex-partner for resolution, which only heightens their distress and isolation.

 For people with an avoidant attachment strategy (distant waves), forgiveness is at odds with their usual tendency of dismissing or suppressing their vulnerable emotions. While they are less likely to dwell on hurtful events than those with an anxious attachment strategy, their lack of emotional engagement might inhibit them from being able to find the much-needed empathy for the other's perspective in order for forgiveness to take place.

Exercise 9.5

As you think about your lost relationship, take a moment to reflect on whether there are things that you might be holding onto in hope of closure in the form of revenge, acknowledgment, understanding, apology or something more.

Are there things you are struggling to let go of? Write them here:

_____

_____

_____

_____

_____

_____

What is it that you are seeking? If this feels unclear, ask yourself: if you got what you are needing, what would that give you or relieve you of emotionally? (For example: *If I got an apology, then I would feel validated. If I felt understood, I could let go of my self-blame.*)

How likely is it that will get this from your lost partner? If it is likely, how could you let them know what you need in clear signals? Write that here. If it is not likely, hang in there...we will help you to find what you need in other ways.

How important is forgiveness in letting go?

Forgiveness is an intentional strategy that interrupts patterns of avoidance and dwelling, decreases negative thoughts and behaviors toward someone who has wronged you, and promotes relationship cohesion[5]. Forgiveness does not mean condoning or excusing bad behavior or minimizing the devastating impact of another's actions.

When appropriate (you are the judge of this) forgiving someone is a transformative process that involves a deliberate and intentional attempt to understand the hurtful event, to take into account the other person's perspective, and to understand the context in which they were hurtful. This means making a concerted effort to understand and empathize with the other and to alter any negative opinions you might be holding about their behavior toward you[6]. Seeing their humanity and acknowledging that good people can make grave mistakes is vital to this process. In a way, finding understanding and empathy for the other person's experience can be a step before forgiveness. This can be a powerful process that is independent from forgiveness but can also help you to move toward forgiveness if that is something that feels important to you.

Exercise 9.6

What have you come to learn about your past relationship and your partner that could help you to be more empathetic toward them?

_____

_____

_____

_____

_____

_____

Only if this feels appropriate for you and your past relationship, using Figure 9.1, write a note to your ex-partner or lost love, reconciling some of the things you want them to know in the interests of forgiving, understanding, and letting go. (Use more paper if needed!)

Dear _____

_____

_____

_____

_____

_____

In the interest of loving & letting go.

Sincerely,

Me ♥

Figure 9.1 Letter to your lost love.

This can be a challenging process, but the benefits of forgiveness can be profound. Forgiveness is associated with a host of positive physical and mental health outcomes such as reduced stress, lower resting heart rate, and greater life satisfaction, as well as having a positive impact on relationship functioning[7].

Now to forgive yourself

It is important to note that *you* deserve the same consideration. We urge you to look at your own actions in your past relationship through the same kind and benign lens so that you might be able to give yourself the gift of empathy and understanding inherent in any forgiveness. We have not met a single person who is not harboring some shameful or guilty feelings about their actions in their relationships. Even though it is excruciating, when we can reflect on the parts of our experience that are hardest to be with, our own guilt and shame, we can learn and grow.

Exercise 9.7

Things that people can feel bad about in relationships:

- How they expressed their frustration.
- How they reacted when feeling fearful or insecure.
- Harsh words or actions that damaged trust between partners.
- Not allowing the other to be themselves.
- Being critical or controlling of the other.
- Feeling threatened by and unaccepting of differences.
- Using someone's vulnerability or weaknesses to hurt them.
- Expecting things from the other that were unreasonable.
- Blaming the other unfairly.
- Curbing the other's freedom.
- Squashing the other's opinions/dreams/goals/beliefs.
- Intimidating or diminishing the other.
- Being rigid and uncompromising.
- Being self-centered.
- Not trying to see the other's point of view.
- Battling to be "right".
- Not responding to the other's attempts to repair or to connect.
- Being unforgiving of mistakes or demanding of perfection.
- Letting other things take priority over the relationship connection.

Looking through this list, tick the things that you are not proud of in your post relationship(s)

List any others or more details about why you are not proud of these actions/omissions:

_____

_____

_____

_____

_____

Can you let yourself really feel the pain of examining your own behavior and holding yourself to account for some of the things you are not proud of? What feelings show up?

_____

_____

_____

Just breathe and let these feelings arrive. This is trauma-growth in action. Letting yourself feel these excruciatingly uncomfortable emotions will help to make sure that you learn and grow from this. This will aid your development and make you an even better person. Remember, only the truly brave and strong can do this.

Exercise 9.8

Now, can you forgive yourself? Can you put your hands on your chest like a loving embrace, breathe, and tell yourself that it is OK to make mistakes, that we all make missteps, that you can learn from this, that this pain is in the service of your growth?

Breathe and feel the warmth of your hands as you give this care to yourself. Sit with this for a few slow, calming breaths.

Can you picture someone safe and supportive, who loves you and is kind to you in your moments of need and pain? (If you struggle to call to mind a special person, you can think of a past attachment figure – like a grandparent – or a spiritual figure, or a pet, or an imagined other).

Who is this person and why are they special to you?

_____

_____

_____

_____

Picture them here with you right now as you do this difficult work.

What would they say to you if they saw your pain and felt your anguish at holding yourself accountable for things you are not proud of?

_____

_____

_____

_____

_____

Can you let that in?

We want you to know that we are proud of you for your willingness to reflect on your role in your past relationships, that you are holding yourself accountable and bravely staying in these difficult emotional places. We know that this will lead to growth for you. We are cheering for you and hoping that you can be kind to yourself in your most vulnerable processing. Please hear our pride and take this in. This is not for the faint of heart and you are doing it. You are earning your security!

Dear Me,

In the interest of self-compassion & forgiveness.

Sincerely,

Me

Figure 9.2 Letter to yourself.

Now, using Figure 9.2, can you write a letter combining your voice with your special person's voice and with ours to soothe and hold the parts that hurt? Can you reach out to yourself with forgiveness? (Use more paper if needed!)

Survival narrative

As you process the loss you have faced and spend time reflecting on hurts in ways that allow for forgiveness of yourself and of your ex-partner, you are undertaking the amazing work of reorganizing your inner world. You are accepting the reality of this loss and reconciling the negative elements of the experience. You are beginning to redefine the relationship and to learn and grow from the lessons learned in it. You are creating a new narrative of this loss and of yourself within this experience that leads to growth.

Hopefully, you are seeing how you lost your way, how your bond was damaged, and how you have survived the loss, and are learning and growing as a result. This hopeful narrative is empowering and restorative. It is imbued with compassion for yourself as an attachment being, a perfectly imperfect human with valid needs. It carries with it lessons from the past and looks to the future with optimism and wisdom. This is amazing, brutal, gut-wrenching, and invigorating work, and we are confident that it will lead you to grow out of this adversity.

Exercise 9.9

The principle of thriving out of adversity is your survival narrative. This is a coherent summary infused with humility, compassion, empathy, and validation, that describes your learnings from this harrowing life event, and allows you to let go and to shift your focus from your rear-vision mirror to the road ahead. Take some time to reflect on how far you have come since Session 1.

What is your survival narrative?

This is not a mantra, it is a summary of where you are now after a good deal of difficult and often painful work.

Write your survival narrative here:

_____

_____

_____

_____

_____

_____

_____

_____

We hope your survival narrative has these elements (see Figure 9.3).

Figure 9.3 Survival narrative.

In this session and in other previous sessions, you are now opening up to new opportunities; opportunities for knowing yourself more deeply and for showing up in your next close relationship in a completely new way. This is a rubber-meets-the-road change in action. It is our sincerest hope that you are now finding a way to make sense of this loss that honors the story of your time together and the contribution you made to that bond but also allows you to move forward in your life and in your relationships with more clarity, comfort, and peace.

Notes

1 Tedeschi, R. G. & Calhoun, L. G. (2004). Posttraumatic growth: Conceptual foundations and empirical evidence. *Psychological Inquiry*, 15 (1), 1–18.
2 Dyrdal, G. M., Røysamb, E., Nes, R. B. & Vitterso, J. (2019). When life happens: Investigating short and long-term effects of life stressors on life satisfaction in a large sample of Norwegian mothers. *Journal of Happiness Studies*, 20, 1689–1715.
3 Guzmán-González, M., Wlodarczyk, A., Contreras, P., Rivera-Ottenberger, D. & Garrido, L. (2019). Romantic attachment and adjustment to separation: The role of forgiveness of the former partner. *Journal of Child and Family Studies*, 28, 3011–3021.
4 Hirst, S. L., Hepper, E. G., & Tenenbaum, H. R. (2019). Attachment dimensions and forgiveness of others: A meta-analysis. *Journal of Social & Personal Relationships*. Online first publication. DOI: 10.1177/0265407519841716
5 Guzmán-González, M., Wlodarczyk, A., Contreras, P., Rivera-Ottenberger, D. & Garrido, L. (2019). Romantic attachment and adjustment to separation: The role of forgiveness of the former partner. *Journal of Child and Family Studies*, 28, 3011–3021.
6 Kimmes, J. G. & Durtschi, J. A. (2016). Forgiveness in romantic relationships: The roles of attachment, empathy and attributions. *Journal of Marital and Family Therapy*, 42 (4), 645–658.
7 Hirst, S. L., Hepper, E. G., & Tenenbaum, H. R. (2019). Attachment dimensions and forgiveness of others: A meta-analysis. *Journal of Social & Personal Relationships*. Online first publication. DOI: 10.1177/0265407519841716

Trusting yourself (again)

Trusting in yourself is a journey that will be so worthwhile! One very common experience of those who have lost a loved one is feeling that you lost trust in yourself while in this relationship or as a result of losing this loved one. Many people ask themselves and professionals like us, how do I get myself back? While it's common for us to hear some version of "time heals all wounds," this phrase is not actually true. If you don't spend this time healing, many people remain defensive, hurting, and mad at their losses. The simple passage of time does not heal wounds, but it can distance us from them. Temporarily, that distance from our pain can be relieving but only in a temporary way. Eventually, our pain gets bigger, takes more and more energy to suppress and ultimately does not stay inside our own skin. As you will have learned from working through this workbook, facing your pain and fear brings you back to yourself.

As you are nearing the end of this workbook, we imagine that you have processed a lot of pain and have started to befriend your fears. We are so proud of you for reaching this point in your healing journey! It has taken a lot of focus and discipline and you have been very dedicated to your healing. We hope you have started to more consistently feel better and can experience the goodness inherent in your healing.

As we continue, in this session, we want to support you in looking at your relationship with yourself. Specifically, about trusting yourself. As a result of a lost relationship, we often realize that we have lost trust with ourselves. Many people report feeling like they lost themselves along the way or at a particular point when the relationship was struggling or when they were working hard to keep their partner happy and their relationship together. Maybe we started focusing too much on our partner. Maybe our partner was not supportive of us focusing on ourselves. Maybe we never had it modeled for us that it is healthy for us to both focus on ourselves as well as give to our partners. Maybe we had thoughts of ending the relationship but were too scared to enact them. Maybe we "knew" that the relationship was not sustainable but we did not want to pay attention to that possibility. There are a lot of possible reasons "why" we might have lost ourselves. But, as we have learned in this workbook, knowing the "why" does not help us resolve the emotional echoes that reside. What is most important is that we process the events that led to us losing trust with ourselves.

Exercise 10.1

When you look back at your relationship and your relationship with yourself, what events decreased your trust in yourself?

_____

_____

_____

_____

_____

DOI: 10.4324/9781003360506-14

How do you feel right now after writing about these pivotal events that eroded your trust in yourself?

_____

_____

_____

_____

_____

_____

What is a good image for how you are feeling right now?

_____

_____

_____

_____

_____

Restoring trust in yourself by listening to your intuition

Most of us do not know how to restore trust with ourselves. We simply go through life with less and less of this most important resource – trusting ourselves – and our life options become limited as a result. Since trust is not a cognitive construct (you cannot tell yourself to trust someone or something that you do not feel trusting of), we need to process the emotions that result from these events where trust was lost. This is the fastest way to restore trust!

Trust in ourselves is often lost when we surprise ourselves by taking action or not by taking action in a key moment, when we do not protect ourselves even when we felt the need to, when we did not speak up even when we felt the need to, we did not take space when needed or when we did not act in our best interest. In these situations, often our "gut-feeling" or intuition might have been plaintively calling out to us and we didn't act on it. All of us have intuition since it is wired into our nervous system. The stem of *intuition* is tueri, the Latin root meaning to guard or protect. The purpose of our intuition is to guard and protect us from danger or to keep us safe. Even with this totally benign purpose – keeping us safe – most of us have an uncertain relationship with our intuition.

Most of us were not raised to pay attention to our intuition. If we did pay attention to it and even validated it, we often were not supported. Our cultures and communities have prioritized cognitive decision making as the "smartest" way to make decisions. While researchers have known this is not the truth, people and communities implore us to be "analytical" as a sign and reflection of our smarts. Year after year of traditional schooling taught us to use our brains solely for the purposes of analyzing in order to make good decisions. Typically, our teachers, coaches, and parents did not tell us that we think with our whole bodies. They did not reflect for us that *our bodies are the foundation for the self.*

The good news in all of this is that your body – this amazing resource designed to keep you safe – is right here, right now. There is nothing else needed for you to have access to the greatest resource you need as a human. Your body holds the answers to your recovery as well as in trusting yourself again. Thankfully, the answer is not to be found in some external thing that you are missing or that you were not given. Trusting yourself is not going to be found outside of yourself. As you know well after completing most of this workbook, trusting yourself comes from finding your own bodily sensations, paying attention to them by listening, and taking action based upon them (again and again). **Find your sensations, pay attention, listen, take action. Repeat.**

Figure 10.1 Losing trust in yourself.

Trusting your felt sense

Your brain is in a constant conversation with your body. This happens typically below and behind your awareness using a feedback loop between your brain and your body called Interoception. Interoception is "the process by which your nervous system senses, interprets, and integrates signals originating from within the body, providing a moment-by-moment mapping of the body's internal landscape across conscious and unconscious levels"[1]. Interoception is happening all the time – even right now – to inform your brain about the state of your safety, comfort, and needs. We share this with you so you have some small idea of what is already happening inside of you to keep you safe and grow your comfort. The great news: *this resource is already working and is always within reach.* The harder part: slowing down, paying attention to it, and making decisions based upon your "felt sense."

For us authors, we each went through a growth process after the break-up of an important relationship. We have shared with each other the moments when we realized that we had to learn the language of our bodies and then we had to risk trusting this "new" language. It was only "new" because nobody had ever shared it before with us. It is actually quite old based on human physiology and evolution. But, that is another book! Right now, your most important task is to look back at the times when you lost trust in yourself. We look back not for you to beat yourself up. We look back to slow ourselves and tune into the process that occurred back then so we can pay attention to what our bodies are telling us now about what happened then. This is how we learn about ourselves and develop our intuition. We listen *now* about *back then.* We listen *now* because our bodies do remember (to ensure our survival... think of the "hot stove" again) and our bodies still hold the intelligence for us. Even years later, our bodies are holding intelligence for our benefit (unprocessed) until we bring it into our awareness.

Exercise 10.2

So, bring to mind one of the situations you wrote about above. Recall your experience and whatever details you can. As you remember and think back, what does your body want you to know?

_____

_____

_____

_____

How does it feel to hear this now (what your body wants you to know)?

_____

_____

_____

_____

_____

Without being hard on yourself, what blocked you from listening and knowing this back then?

_____

_____

_____

_____

_____

As you work through this exercise, notice what it feels like. Usually, people report relief with this exercise. Although it is hard to go back and remember again, there is relief in finding, naming, and absorbing and integrating the intelligence that your body has been holding for you.

Write a list of your pivotal life events that you can return to in order to remember key moments and glean the intelligence your body has held for you:

_____

_____

_____

_____

_____

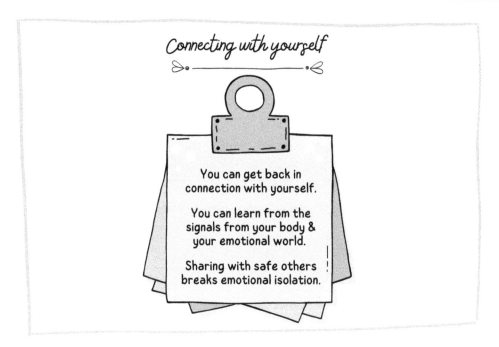

Figure 10.2 Connecting with yourself.

When you can, share your body's intelligence with a close friend or family member with whom you feel safe. How was it to share?

_____

_____

_____

_____

_____

_____

Although new and different to share, we are so glad you took the risk in sharing. It is important to regularly open up and share with safe others. It is a great habit to practice since it breaks your emotional isolation, which is so costly to humans!

What to do with your inner-critic

All of us have an inner-critic. That is the good news and the bad news! The origin of your inner-critic was all about keeping you safe. When relationships did not provide enough protection or safety for you, you had to develop a method of protecting yourself to ensure your survival. For most of us, when we do something or behave in a way that brings forth our own shame (see Session 5 for more on shame), being critical of ourselves is protective. Much like, "if I really criticize myself, then it won't hurt as much when someone else notices my awfulness" or "if I am really mad at myself and feel really bad, then I won't mess up like this again." Our shame has a voice embedded in it which gets louder and more persistent in order to keep us from taking a relationship risk when a relationship risk could lead to further exposure and rejection. This voice constantly reminds us of our humanity...especially our flaws and the mistakes we have made. All humans make mistakes regularly, but in our developmental years, the mistakes we made and how others reacted to them became a template for our shame. *The voice of our shame became our inner-critic that lives with us like an unwanted houseguest that we can't quite bring ourselves to evict.*

Figure 10.3 Inner-critic.

Exercise 10.3

Most of us do not want to get to know our inner-critic, which is understandable. But, as with all phenomena based on emotion, when something important to our survival does not get processed, it grows and takes up more space inside of us. Eventually, these unprocessed events solidify and become our defenses and fuel the voice of our inner-critic. Defenses, of course, make intimacy harder, as you have learned throughout this workbook. In order to break this vicious cycle, let us help you make friends with your inner-critic! It will not be as painful as it sounds right now, we promise.

When you hear the voice of your inner-critic, what is an image for it?

_____

_____

_____

_____

_____

And a good name for it? _____

What are its most common messages for you?

_____

_____

_____

_____

_____

And, how have you typically responded to these messages?

_____

_____

_____

_____

_____

_____

And, how have your typical responses left you feeling?

_____

_____

_____

_____

_____

_____

If someone (like us!) says to let yourself challenge or protest against your inner-critic, what kind of protest would you express? Are you the kind of protester who makes a sign and pickets? If so, what words would you put on your sign? "Stop it!" "Be QUIET!" "(Name of Critic) not welcome here!!!" Maybe your protest is a written argument. If so, what would you write to argue the voice of your inner-critic?

_____

_____

_____

_____

_____

_____

Maybe you prefer to be heard – literally – and you want to use your voice to protest. What does your voice want to say?

_____

_____

_____

_____

_____

_____

Does it want to yell? Use sign-language? Use silence to make your points?

_____

_____

_____

_____

_____

Exercise 10.4

When we externalize our inner-critics in these ways, we are wedging ourselves between our core selves and the echoes of our shame. Remember back in Session Five and the image of the glasses...when our shame goes unchecked, it can become the lens through which we see all of life. **We think our shame is us.** When we name our critic, talk to it, and protest its messages to us, we are creating space between it and us. We are containing, distancing, and shrinking it (putting it back into the small space it was originally meant to have).

Interestingly, how would it be to ask your inner-critic what its purpose has been all these years?

What function has it been trying to serve?

_____

_____

_____

_____

_____

_____

And, lastly, what does it need in order to shrink, stay contained, and leave you alone?

_____

_____

_____

_____

_____

_____

Befriending yourself

Restoring a relationship with your intuition is the foundation of trusting yourself. Remember, you cannot tell yourself to trust something or someone that you do not feel trusting of since trust is not a cognitive construct. To feel trusting, you must *feel* trusting. Meaning, you need to develop a relationship with your own intuition so it can provide the protection it has always been meant to provide for you!

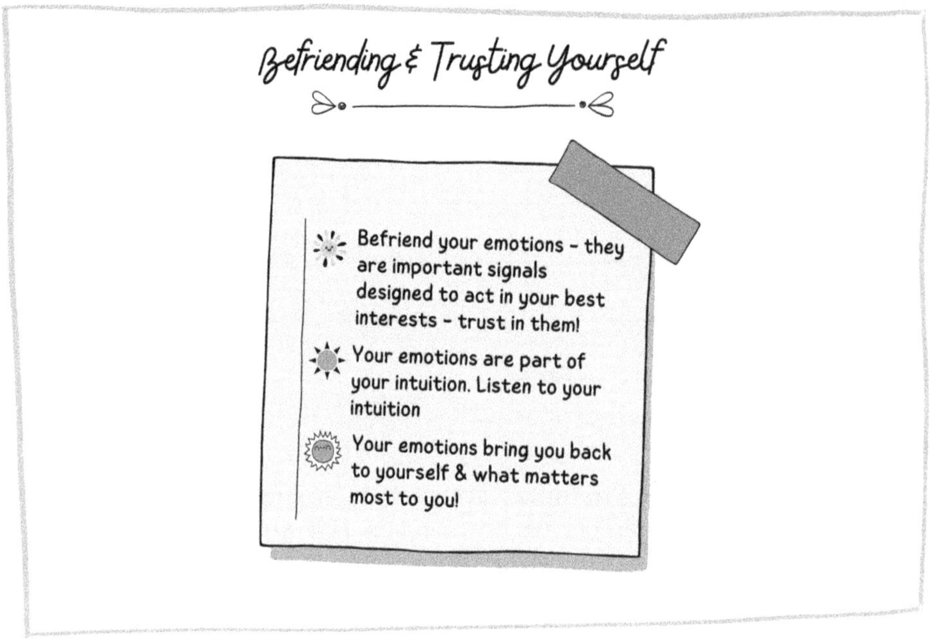

Figure 10.4 Befriending and trusting yourself.

Befriending yourself, especially your feelings, reorients you to your best life again and again. Trusting yourself grows implicitly as you return to your emotion!

As we wrap up this session, we want to remind you that the clearest sign of healing is you trusting yourself again. You knowing and trusting your own emotions again or, perhaps, for the first time is our shared goal in writing this workbook. We strongly encourage you to develop a daily practice of finding your feelings. Much like exercise, healthy eating, and other good habits, we want to encourage you to make it a habit to pay attention to the signals your body gives you. Slow down and focus on them. What is their emotional message? Does your body get tense, give you the chills, or tighten your throat? Make space for the feelings that come with your bodily sensations. This, after all, is your intuition working to ensure your safety! Feeling your feelings always brings us back to ourselves and what matters most to us!

Note

1   Khalsa, S. S., Adolphs, R., Cameron, O. G., Critchley, H. D., Davenport, P. W., Feinstein, J. S., et al., Interoception and Mental Health: A Road Map. *Biological Psychiatry: Cognitive Neuroscience and Neuroimaging*. June 2018; 3: 501–513.

Building security with others

As we near the end of this workbook, we want you to pause here for a moment and take in how far you have come. This work is extremely difficult and we are full of admiration for your grit in working through these exercises with us. In this session, we will look at how to bring your insights about your past relationships, your attachment strategies, and your emotional awareness into your next relationship. This is an exciting place, ripe with opportunities for shaping the kind of loving connections you are wanting (and that you deserve).

To start this process, we will explore the beliefs and expectations that you might be carrying with you into your next big love relationship. These are the blueprints you have developed over your lifetime – the accumulation of all your experiences in past close relationships. We will look at the beliefs that helped you to shape security in your loving relationships and which ones set you up for potential struggles. Then, we will help you to bravely walk back onto the playing field of romantic love with your inner security waving like a banner!

Importantly, we will also investigate how to detect secure attachment strategies in others to be sure that you set off in new relationships on the right foot. You can *now* create the relationship you want, so we will focus on *how* to shape the security that you are seeking in your new emotional bonds. We will take all you have learned about yourself and your deepest needs, and help you to honor these as you consider entering a new relationship. We will look at how to spot and avoid unhelpful dynamics in relationships, and how to earn security together as you create a loving bond with someone special.

Beliefs and expectations about relationships

We all hold beliefs about the value of close relationships and our fundamental lovability. These can either help or hinder our attempts to find love. As you work to release yourself from the emotional ties to your former partner and look toward the idea of embarking on new connections moving forward, it might pay to be aware of the expectations or biases about relationships you could be carrying with you. Sometimes, these expectations can become self-fulfilling prophecies that, without awareness, can live unchallenged within us, and can cause us to perpetuate past negative patterns in future relationships. We do not want that for you!

Exercise 11.1

Our lived experiences of turning to our attachment figures during times of need offer powerful learnings that we store away in the form of "working models."[1] We have two key working models that relate to our attachment needs, they are a *model of other* and a *model of self*. These models provide a template or set of expectations for what it means to turn to another in times of need, and what we can expect from this (model of other) as well as about our own self-worth and lovability (model of self). We develop positive ideas about the value of turning to others and our worthiness of love and support when our close relationship have shown us this.

Positive Model of Other:

- I know my attachment figures are there for me when I need them.
- If I signal, they will respond to me.
- Sharing my worries, fears, and joys with them makes me feel better.
- I can trust them not to intentionally hurt me.
- I can count on them for comfort and encouragement.

DOI: 10.4324/9781003360506-15

Positive Model of Self:

• I am worthy of love and support.
• My feelings make sense.
• I can manage tough situations.
• I deserve comfort and encouragement.
• I can signal my needs.

Being aware of your own thoughts and expectations in close relationships is extremely helpful in getting to know yourself better, and represents an important step in being able to move out of old relational patterns when your attachment alarms go off (as they inevitably do for us all). When a person has experiences with inaccessible, unresponsive, and disengaged attachment figures, instead of developing a positive model of other and model of self, they develop *negative* beliefs about relationships understandably.

In Figure 11.1, take a moment to consider what your beliefs are about the value of close relationships and your own worthiness of love and support. Mark along the two lines for where you best fit.

We know from previous research that people with *secure* attachment strategies have generally experienced their caregivers as sensitive and responsive, so they are likely to form positive beliefs about close relationships, and to have developed a healthy sense of self. They bring these open and positive ideas with them into their relationships, which means that they are more likely to see their partner in a positive light, to feel confident about their partner's reliability, and to feel worthy of love and support.

 Given that people with an *anxious* attachment strategy are likely to have experienced their caregivers as inconsistently available, they can hold more complex or even negative views of others' reliability in their adult relationships, and to doubt their own lovability. Sadly, people with an anxious attachment strategy are quite susceptible to blaming themselves for their attachment figure's lack of reliability. Despite their fears of abandonment and self-doubt, they generally believe that it is easy to fall in love, and remain hopeful about this.

People with an *avoidant* attachment strategy are more likely to doubt that romantic love happens, or even exists. They carry with them more cynical beliefs about relationships, and pre-emptively conclude that others cannot be relied on, and do not have positive intentions.

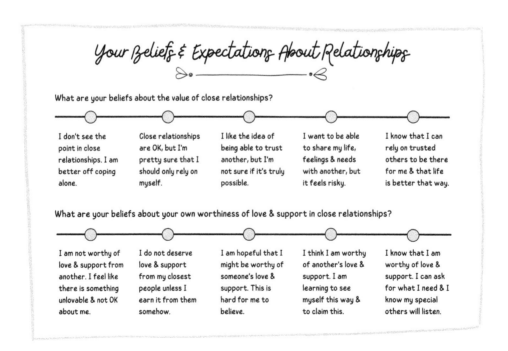

Figure *11.1* Beliefs about relationships and worthiness of love.

This arises from the cumulative effect of experiencing their early caregivers as rejecting or dismissive of their attachment needs. They have learned that it is better to cope alone, and to suppress their painful emotions, rather than risk turning to an unresponsive or rejecting caregiver. As adults, people with an avoidant attachment strategy are not likely to take their emotional needs to another, or even to acknowledge them to themselves.

 People with a *hybrid* attachment strategy (fearful-avoidant) are likely to have experienced early attachment relationships as frightening and dangerous as well as inconsistent and often confusing. This, understandably, leaves a powerful mark on your trust in turning to others in times of need and joy. As adults, people with a hybrid attachment strategy are likely to oscillate between seeking closeness in the hope that it will be safe, but then to become fearful of being hurt because this is what they have learned to expect from relationships. This leaves them wary of connection and contributes to their mixed signals (push-pull) to loved ones.

Exercise 11.2

We hope that it is becoming a little clearer how the beliefs we bring with us into our close relationships can become self-perpetuating, often without our conscious awareness. Take a moment to reflect on the beliefs about others' responsiveness and your lovability that you might be carrying with you into your next close relationship.

What did you learn about close relationships from your earliest attachment relationships?

_____

_____

_____

_____

_____

How have your subsequent relationships throughout your life confirmed or revised these views of others and yourself?

_____

_____

_____

_____

_____

| Big Waves | Distant Waves | Hybrid Waves | Riding the Waves |

Figure 11.2 After reading the descriptions above, circle the "wave style" (attachment strategy) that best describes your beliefs and expectations about close relationships.

How have these beliefs and experiences impacted you? How do they show up in relationships?

_____

_____

_____

_____

_____

Earned security

Coming to understand where and what you learned about relationships and your own worth, means that you are taking important steps in building your self-awareness and revising your views of others and yourself. As we know, self-awareness involves tuning into your inner world, _and_ zooming out to see the bigger patterns in your life. It means listening to your deepest needs, and intentionally letting them guide your life direction and your interactions with others. Knowing yourself in this way allows you to be a resource for yourself, and to draw on others as a resource as well. It lets you know when you have stepped away from what matters to you, or when you might be actively suppressing your needs. These awarenesses are key to being able to intentionally make changes for the better. John Bowlby called this "earned security" and it is a beautiful reminder to us all that we can grow and develop secure attachment "in relationship" with ourselves and with safe others even in adulthood.

Exercise 11.3

Here are some healthy beliefs that people can carry into their loving relationships. Tick the ones the resonate with you:

- I can turn to others for support and encouragement when I need it.
- Others will care about my feelings.
- My person will never intentionally hurt me.
- It helps me to share my struggles with a trusted other.
- I am entitled to my emotions and needs.
- My partner and I are respectful of our differences.
- I can trust my partner not to use my vulnerabilities against me.
- It is OK to be me within this relationship.
- I have a responsibility to hold my partner's vulnerabilities gently.
- It is my responsibility to manage my own reactivity so that I am safe for my partner.
- I am entitled to feel safe in this relationship.
- I am loveable just as I am.
- I accept my person's humanity.
- We give each other grace when we misstep.
- We can laugh, cry, rejoice, rupture, and repair together.
- We keep our promises to each other.

After reading through these healthy beliefs, which ones, of all those you selected, would you like to be most prominent in your next close relationship? Do you have more you would like to add?

_____

_____

_____

_____

_____

_____

_____

Do you now feel worthy of this (we certainly hope so!)? Why? Or, if not, why not?

_____

_____

_____

_____

What are your "non-negotiables" when entering into another close relationship? This is a commitment to yourself e.g. *"I will never again feel afraid to express my needs or opinions with my partner. I am worthy of love and support. I am allowed to be my own person. I will not accept a relationship that makes me feel afraid or less-than."*

_____

_____

_____

_____

_____

_____

_____

Read this again…this matters!

What do you need to do to remain connected to *yourself* in your next relationship? Tick the ones that apply and add your own.

- Pay attention to my inner world.
- Do not ignore red flags.
- Remind myself of my non-negotiables regularly.
- Ask a friend to hold me accountable.
- Notice myself making excuses for my needs not being met.
- Treat myself with compassion and empathy.
- More: _____

_____

_____

_____

_____

Intentionally leading with security in your next relationship

It is our hope that becoming aware of your attachment strategy has helped you to see how it might have impacted the way you have shown up in relationships, and built an awareness of what might have been missing for you in your earliest attachment relationships, as well as your adult relationships. Be compassionate with yourself as we all continue to learn about ourselves and our impacts while we grow through adulthood. For most of us, nobody taught us about this type of awareness before!

Exercise 11.4

How do your expectations about close relationships impact how you approach them? For instance, if you struggle to see the value in close relationships, you might be reluctant to reach out. If you doubt your own worthiness of love, you might try too hard to please others.

_____

_____

_____

_____

_____

_____

Through working through the exercises in this book, we hope that you can see how the way you have been attempting to get your needs met in close relationships might have actually contributed to some of the insecurity in your previous relationships. This knowledge tells you exactly what you need to work on in future relationships to take responsibility for your half of the connection. This is empowering! You can now create the relationship you want. You send clearer signals about your needs so that they have a chance of being met.

Let us reflect on what you want to do differently in your next relationship. Think about how you would like to show up in your next relationship, how you want to manage your emotions, how you want to signal your needs and how you want to respond to your partner.

Instead of reacting with my "old" coping strategy (name old coping strategy):

_____

_____

_____

I would like to do: _____

_____

_____

_____

When I feel strong emotions (especially fear or anger), I would like to respond to them by:

_____

_____

When I need something from my partner, I can now signal this by: _____

_____

_____

_____

Notice how different this is from your "old" ways of managing attachment-related emotions. This is important progress!

Remember, sending clear signals of vulnerability and need between people who care about each other is the royal road to secure connection. When you can do this, you are doing your part to ensure that you have a secure and healthy bond in your next close relationship (and all your close relationships). You are waving your inner security like a banner!

Exercise 11.5

You have done the work to reflect on your role in the attachment security in your closest relationships. This is valuable and meaningful work that we know will serve you well moving forward. However, you are only responsible for 50% of the connection with a special other. So what signs might indicate attachment security in a potential partner?

Take a look at the points on Figure 11.3 Relationship red and green flags.

What "green flags" stand out to you as qualities you would love to see in a potential partner?

_____

_____

_____

_____

_____

_____

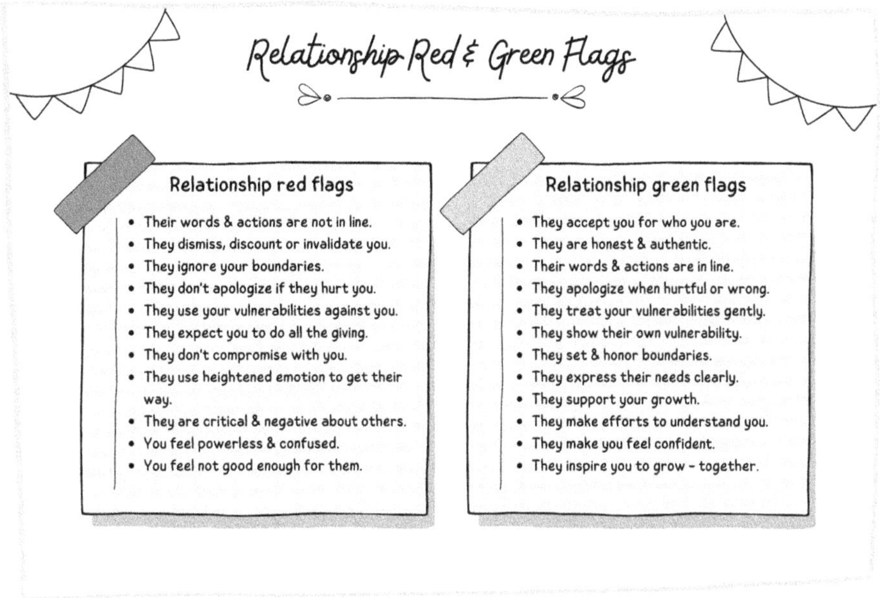

Relationship Red & Green Flags

Relationship red flags
- Their words & actions are not in line.
- They dismiss, discount or invalidate you.
- They ignore your boundaries.
- They don't apologize if they hurt you.
- They use your vulnerabilities against you.
- They expect you to do all the giving.
- They don't compromise with you.
- They use heightened emotion to get their way.
- They are critical & negative about others.
- You feel powerless & confused.
- You feel not good enough for them.

Relationship green flags
- They accept you for who you are.
- They are honest & authentic.
- Their words & actions are in line.
- They apologize when hurtful or wrong.
- They treat your vulnerabilities gently.
- They show their own vulnerability.
- They set & honor boundaries.
- They express their needs clearly.
- They support your growth.
- They make efforts to understand you.
- They make you feel confident.
- They inspire you to grow – together.

Figure 11.3 Relationship red and green flags.

Why are these important to you?

_____

_____

_____

_____

What "red flags" stand out to you as qualities you would like to avoid in a potential partner?

_____

_____

_____

_____

Why are these of concern to you?

_____

_____

_____

_____

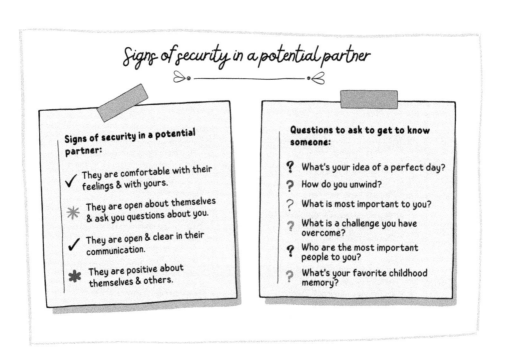

Figure 11.4 Signs of security in a potential partner.

Building a secure bond with someone special to you

We want to take a moment to explore how to build a bond together, so that you can start out on a great path in your next relationship that will set you up to earn security together. Remember, all partners in close relationships typically need to feel accepted, supported, and understood as well as feeling loved, appreciated, and important. These are such normal needs, and having them met in a healthy and mutually satisfying relationship, enhances our physical and mental health.

Building a bond is achieved through mutual sharing and emotional responsiveness. This means opening up to each other, and greeting each other with understanding and compassion. As you might recall from earlier sessions, a secure attachment figure is accessible, responsive, and engaged; they are there when you need them, they offer comfort and support, and they care about you. Any time partners can take their vulnerable feelings to the special other and are greeted with warmth, reassurance, and comfort, the bond is strengthened. Each time you risk revealing another part of yourself (intentionally or unintentionally) to your partner, and they respond with acceptance and compassion, the more your trust and self-confidence grows as does the strength and security of your bond with each other. Each time you signal for them in a time of need, and they hear your call and reach back, you know you can rely on them and that you are safe with them.

In this way, your attachment bond gradually develops through large and small reaches and risks, leaps of faith that are proven to be safe. These are the ways that secure attachment strategies lead to the building of a secure attachment bond.

Exercise 11.6

How could you offer comfort to your partner when they are feeling vulnerable?

What do you need from your partner to feel comforted when you are vulnerable?

How could your partner best support and encourage you when you are feeling uncertain?

How could you show your support and encouragement for your partner's dreams?

_____

_____

_____

_____

_____

Exercise 11.7

When you find yourself embarking on a new love relationship, as the security of your new bond is growing, try not to panic when there are hits and misses along the way. In all relationships, there are hits and misses. The process of coming to interpret each other's signals and understand each other's needs can definitely be bumpy! There is no way you can automatically *know* or intuit exactly what your partner needs on an attachment level nor they for you. You can take a guess based on what we broadly know humans need to feel securely connected to another, but as you know, this can vary between people depending on their individual encounters with attachment figures throughout their lives. Our particular attachment strategies and our experiences in close relationships, impact how we ask for our attachment needs (or not), and the types of things that set off our attachment alarms.

When a bond is forming we *help* the other to be a source of comfort and support by telling them what we are needing, rather than expecting them to just *know*. This is where clear signals of need really help to remove ambiguity. Remember, the more you are paying attention to your own inner emotional world, the more you will know about your deepest fears and needs. This knowledge is invaluable in being able to share clearly with your new partner, when it feels right to do so.

The sending and receiving of clear emotional signals like this is the most effective way to build a strong bond. It also is an effective way to repair a frayed bond after a moment of disconnection, or a relational hurt. In attachment language, we call these moments attachment "ruptures." If an attachment bond is like a beautiful silk rope, made of many interwoven threads that give it its strength, then an attachment rupture is an event that tears some of these threads. We know that rupture and repair is a normal, expectable part of developing and maintaining a secure attachment bond. We suggest

Figure 11.5 Reminder: Path to security.

greeting ruptures as opportunities for strengthening understanding between you both. Try to see the repair of each rupture as adding more threads to your rope together – making it stronger. There is a literal reality to becoming stronger in our broken places!

What do you need to work on so that you can send clear, non-triggering signals to your person when you need them?

_____

_____

_____

_____

_____

_____

Here are some suggestions for managing ruptures or stuck spots with your new partner. Tick those that you have learned throughout your work in this book that you could now try:

- Tune into your emotional world.
- Breathe slowly and smoothly.
- Give yourself care and compassion – it hurts to feel disconnected.
- Ask yourself what you are needing or intending at a heart-level.
- Send a clear message from your heart.
- Tune into what could be happening for the other.
- Access empathy and compassion for the other – this hurts them too.
- Listen to the attachment message in the other's emotion.
- Slow down when emotions are escalating and signals are becoming scrambled.
- Lead with your vulnerability.
- Take responsibility for your part of the disconnection or misattunement.
- Commit to being an emotionally safe partner.

More: _____

_____

_____

_____

_____

_____

_____

_____

You are now on your way to cultivating a new way of being in love! As a result of your hard work in this session (and in all the previous sessions), your future love relationships will feel better to you and your future partners! You now have new ways of understanding your distress and you have learned the importance of sending clear emotional signals which are vital to having attachment security with each other. You have learned how to slow down in emotionally intense moments and how to lead by

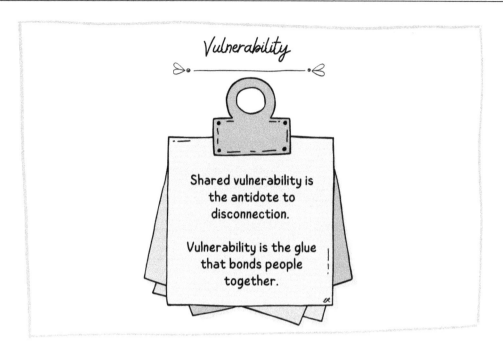

Figure 11.6 Vulnerability is the antidote.

sharing your vulnerabilities. These new skills will serve you so well and offer a new type of protection to your heart. Although loving another is risky for all of us, risking love with these new ways of clarifying your needs and protecting your heart by seeking attachment security will serve you in your years and decades to come!

Note

1   Bowlby, J. (1969/1982). *Attachment and Loss: Volume 1 Attachment.* New York, NY: Basic Books.

Maintaining your momentum

You have made it! You have done it. Congratulations! Making it to this final chapter is amazing and reflects so well on you and your commitment to heal. We are so happy for you!

In this final session, we want to reflect your accomplishments. All of us need to know the specifics of what we have been doing, especially when doing well. The world is so good at highlighting our mistakes. Here, with you, we want to highlight your successes!

Look how far you have come

In Session One, you readied yourself for this journey. You named your "wave style" – the typical way you processed your emotions. That was such an important initial step to getting to know your inner world. Then, you highlighted the healthy ways you nurture and take care of yourself. We hope you have continued to do those healthy, soothing things that you feel so supported by! And then you gave yourself permission – remember that? Writing a permission note to yourself to…feel? To speak? To take time away? Think back to what *you gave yourself permission to pay attention to, to feel, and to speak about!* This is such a vital step in making changes for the better.

Session Two was all about reviewing your most recent relationship – the hardest part of all is to look back at your lost love. You were so strong to name specifics of that relationship – what happened that you do not feel good about and, of course, positive contributions you made to that relationship. It was in this session that we started talking about why it hurts so much to lose a love relationship and the safe people in your life that have helped you hold your hurt. It was here that we started orienting you to the strength required to be vulnerable. Starting a relationship with your own vulnerability was amazing! *We know there is no greater gift you can continue to give yourself than staying with your own humanity, your own vulnerability, even when it is uncomfortable.* Way to go, friend!

We focused on your relationship's interactional pattern in Session Three. We hope you found clarity in the pattern you became caught in with this lost special someone so that you can bring this clarity into your next relationships. Your clarity about your past love *will* help you in future love relationships! Knowing your steps in the past relationship cycle will assist you in all your future relationships. Knowing your steps will also be a benefit to your next partner. Whether your wave style was to turn up the emotional heat or to try to turn it down, this clarity will make those upsetting moments in your next relationship even easier to navigate. As a part of this process, you also came to know and name your longings. Longings are so important to pay attention to. If they go unmet, for too long, our hearts start shutting down which is the first way we impact our love relationship and our partner. Naming our longings helps us get clarity about our needs. Remember your needs? So important – not so we can make demands but so we can check-in and *ask ourselves if this next relationship is meeting our needs and longings.*

Session Four was all about learning your attachment strategy. Remember, your initial wave pattern reflected your typical way of processing your emotions? In Session Four, we connected this wave style with your attachment strategy that grew in your nervous system as you grew up and became an adult. Based on the responsiveness of our parents and caregivers, you either coped with their non-responsiveness by turning up your emotional signals (in order to get their attention!) or by turning off your emotional signals (in order not to draw attention to yourself). Some of us combined these two possibilities which created a hybrid way of coping – in one moment, I turned up the emotion and, in the next moment, I coped by turning it down and going quiet. This is a really big learning for each of

DOI: 10.4324/9781003360506-16

us for our future love relationships! *Knowing how you typically cope – with your emotion and attachment relationships – makes your relationship predictable and trustworthy!*

Session Five started Part Two of this journey. In Session Five, our focus was on gently, kindly helping you find your fear. And, the importance of finding your fear! We would never suggest you spend precious time doing something that is not necessary or relevant. *The "why" behind facing our fear is just as important as the "how" we best face our fears.* In this session you sorted out your relationship with your own fear, especially when that fear was unwanted, perhaps judged to be unwarranted, and certainly inconvenient. Having an ongoing relationship with your fear is the most efficient way of keeping yourself (and your loved ones) safe and thriving! It seems paradoxical, but it's true. *Knowing our fear, referencing our fear as it comes alive is the best way to ensure your safety. Sharing it with a safe other makes it all the more potent!*

Helping you befriend your anger was the focus of Session Six. Anger – one of the biggest emotions humans have – can be hard to get close to but, after all, your anger has important messages embedded in it. Did you realize the important messages of protest and protection that your anger holds? We focused on the function of your anger, how your "wave style" or attachment strategy influences your relationship with your own and other people's anger and the potential build-up of resentment. We taught you the important difference between secondary (fast-moving, reactive anger) and primary (non-blaming, vulnerable anger) anger and helped you name the common triggers of your anger. When you look back at the exercises you completed in Session Six, we hope you see your courage to get to know your anger. We hope you see how *knowing your anger is a key to understanding the protest voice embedded within your anger.* Pay attention to the voice of your protest embedded in your anger!

Session Seven was all about emotional scars and how these emotional scars function in similar ways as physical scars. Scars result from wounds that heal or are in the process of healing. While a sign of healing, scars are an imprint that reminds us of our suffering. Emotional scars are usually invisible but are potent nonetheless. If we do not know and pay attention to our emotional scars, they seem to grow, spread out a bit, and take up more space than they did initially, perhaps. They are easily bumped and are exquisitely painful. All scars have memories associated with them. Memories that leave emotional scars do not fade like other memories do, unfortunately. This is why, in Session Seven, you spent precious time naming what led to your emotional scars. This was hard work! And, you did it! Remembering your "wave style" (attachment strategy) will continue to assist you in knowing what is most helpful to you in working with your emotional scars. *It takes a lot of strength to name what hurt you and then share it with a safe other.* This was such an important step in your healing and we are so proud that you did it!

In Session Eight, we started the deep dive into grief and loss. It is always so hard to turn and face our grief especially when losing a primary relationship. The fabric of your life was torn and left tattered. Session 8 focused on two key components of the grieving process: disorganization and despair. As you worked through the exercises in Session Eight, you felt the sting of realizing your new reality was not going to include your special someone, your hope to reconcile with this special person faded away, and it felt like your world turned upside down. This is a lot to process and make sense of for you (for anyone). But, you made it through by learning about and focusing on healthy grief or, also known as, successful grief. It will continue to be important that you remind yourself that grief is a process that has a beginning, middle and end. That is right, *grief does have an ending, but you will find your way there in your own way, at your own pace.* As a result of working through Session Eight, the intensity of your grief has decreased, you have found healthy ways to grieve that work for you, and you are closer to the end of the intense grieving phase. We send you our warmest congratulations for making it through this most intense process.

Part Three of our workbook included Sessions Nine, Ten and Eleven where we start to look to the future. In Session Nine, we focused on forgiveness and letting go. Despite all the pain and hardships you have suffered as a result of your loss, there is also opportunity. We do not write that with levity. We know that you have earned the opportunities of your loss because you faced your loss and you processed it. It is in the processing of it that new meaning – many times, positive meaning – can be made. Transformation happens as a result of doing the hard work of processing your grief and pain. This transformation allows for new possibilities to take root by immersing yourself in your experience rather than wallowing. *Immersing leads to transformation; wallowing keeps us stuck and not transforming.* Tracking your closeness or distance to your grief – knowing and remembering your wave style – will help you know when you are immersing yourself. Letting go is an active process that can take some repetition especially as you work your way toward forgiveness. You might have written your lost love an important letter about how this process is going for you. *It is so important that you be gracious with yourself – track your letting go and forgiveness with a lot of compassion and remind yourself that repetition is healthy!*

We brought your focus back to you in Session Ten by highlighting the importance of building trust with yourself after the loss of this important relationship. For some of us, it has been about restoring your trust in yourself. For others, it will be the first time in your adult life that you focused on building trust with yourself. Either option is okay. Any significant loss will throw us for a loop. We will wonder what we missed. We might question why we did not want to pay attention to the warning signs we saw. Restoring trust is all about getting back into relationship with your felt-sense, your emotion. Remember that emotion is our signaling system. *Building trust means slowing down and paying attention to your emotions and what they may be signaling to you.* Felt-sense and emotions are part of our intuition. In Session Ten, you learned that our intuition is meant to protect and guard and the process of interoception is how our intuition and emotion signal to us. Learning to go closer to your inner critic was also a key element of Session Ten. We all have an inner critic whose origins were all about keeping us safe and alive. But, often our inner critics take too much liberty and they become too big and too hard on us. *We need to go closer to them to contain, tame, and shrink the potency of our inner critic.* We need to get our inner critics to mellow out and Session Ten included this important process!

The focus of Session 11 was all about creating your next *secure* relationship! We started with helping you to clarify your beliefs and expectations about relationships. This important need – to know your own beliefs and expectations – is backed by science. *Remember, the responsiveness of our early caregivers wired us for security or insecurity.* Those of us with responsive parents, developed attachment security which predisposes us to positive views of other and self. Those of us with inconsistent parenting developed insecure attachment which predisposes us to negative views of other and self. Remember, that even with unpredictable parental and caregiver responsiveness, *we can always earn attachment security with ourselves and with those most special to us.* Through processes like this workbook, we each have the opportunity to revise our views of other and self into more positive views! Attachment is a dynamic force which means we can always revise it. Staying connected to yourself, even while in your next relationship, is one of the key messages of Session 11.

Let us celebrate!

Now that you are at the end of this workbook, our hope is that you have felt supported and comforted in your loss, that you have grown in knowledge and experience about your attachment strategy and healthy relationships, and that you will have felt the relief after feeling into your own pain, fear, and needs in order to befriend your emotional world. In this final session, we want to celebrate with you! We will help you to reflect on how far you have come and what you want to keep working on.

Exercise 12.1

As for all of us, our self-development is a constantly evolving process. What is different now for you?

_____

_____

_____

_____

_____

_____

Dear Future Me,

_____

_____

_____

_____

In the interest of staying connected to ME,

Sincerely,

Me ♥

Figure 12.1 Letter to your future self.

As an important reflection, take a few minutes now to write a letter to your future self. Tell your future self what you have learned about yourself. What feels different about you now? What are your commitments to yourself going forward into your next relationships? How will you stay connected to your own emotions in order to build and maintain trust with yourself?

You will want to read and re-read your letter to your future self many times! Keep it in a place where you can find it easily in your moments of doubt, pain, and fear. Use it to reassure yourself of your goodness, your growth, and your commitments to yourself for all of your future relationships!

Exercise 12.2

Now that you are connecting with yourself and the ideas, beliefs and values that you want to hold onto as you move forward in your life, we know that (as for all of us) there will inevitably be times when you encounter pain, self-doubt, rejection, or worse. We invite you to prepare for these moments by reflecting on what words of advice and comfort your older, wiser, "future-self" might have for you. Just as you now can think of comfort that you could offer your past-self in times of pain, we are hoping that you might be able to offer yourself comfort should you falter or lose your balance in the future. These times happen to us all and how we greet ourselves in our vulnerability often makes the difference between adding to our suffering or honoring our resilience. We really want to see you honoring your beauty, strength, and humanity. We want to see you befriend your inner world and be a source of comfort for yourself in your rawest of moments.

We invite you to write a letter *from* your future-self – someone who is content with their direction in life, who is not perfect, but who is wise and kind to themselves. What might your future self say to you *now* when you are hurting? What words of encouragement might they have for you? How might they offer you comfort? What would they remind you of when your self-belief seems far out of reach? When the world seems against you and your pain feels overwhelming?

Keep this somewhere safe and read it whenever you are feeling wobbly and uncertain. This acts as a hug from the most important person in your world and the one who knows you best!

Dear Younger Me,

You've got this. I'm here with you.

Sincerely,

Older wiser Me ♥

Figure 12.2 Letter from your older, wiser self.

One final reflection from us

Maybe you have noticed. Maybe you have wondered. Maybe you had a thought to yourself that session by session, this process is starting to feel familiar. These sessions have a similar flow as each other. These exercises have a similar rhythm as the others. *Well…it is true!* Each session has a flow that is similar to the other sessions. Each exercise has the same, now-familiar elements. Generally, there have been five components embedded in the exercises used throughout this workbook! Here are those elements:

1. Get curious about your inner world. Regularly pay attention to how you are feeling. When a feeling shows up, **notice and name it**.
2. Pay attention to your feeling, find where it lives in your body. What is the sensation of it? Breathe into it. Experience it. Let yourself actually **feel** it.
3. Ask yourself what this feeling might be telling you about something you need. Find the **meaning**, message, and the wisdom in this experience.
4. Acknowledge the meaning and the **significance** of this emotion to yourself – even if it seems small. Share it with a safe other or a loved one.
5. Notice how you feel after **acknowledging** your feelings and **sharing** them with someone important to you.

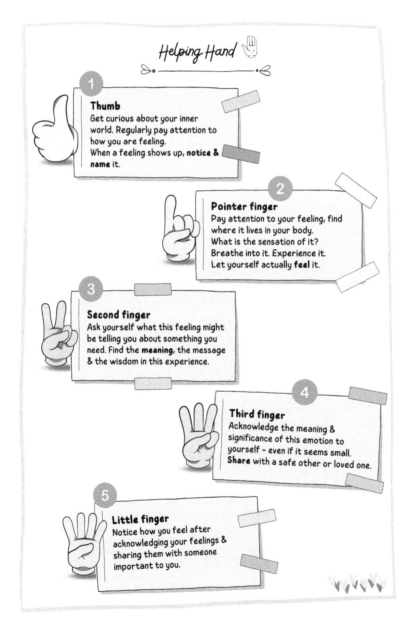

Figure 12.3 Helping hand.

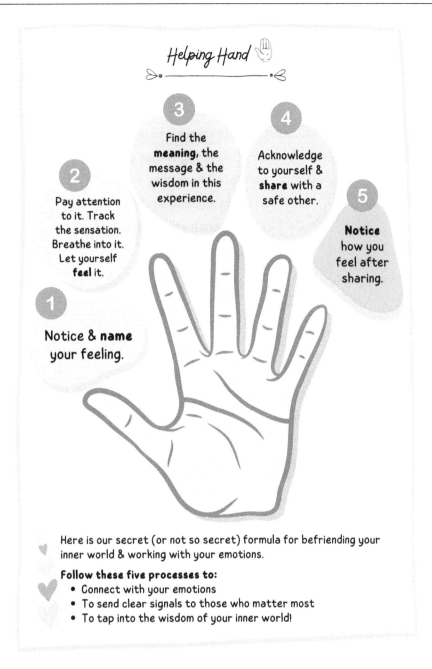

Figure 12.4 Helping hand summary.

Our hopes for you ♥

Well, here you are at the very end of this book! It is our most heartfelt hope that you have felt supported as you have worked through the process of honoring your pain, accepting and learning from your loss, and have emerged stronger for this labor. We hope that we have been able to offer you a hand to hold in the dark, and some comfort in your vulnerability. We hope that you are seeing some light now, light that is emanating from your very bright future. We hope that you will take all this knowledge about attachment, emotion, relationships, and your beautiful self forward into a life of self-acceptance and secure bonding with the special people in your life. That is our wish for you and for all of us; all imperfect humans trying to find our way with those who matter most to us. Now, instead of looking back to find answers, when you look back, all you will see is how far you have come. Go and be brave and love openly! You can do it and you deserve it!

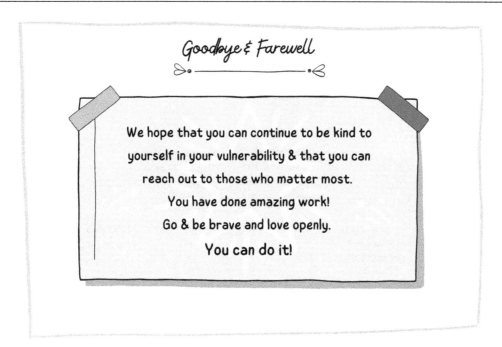

Figure 12.5 Goodbye and farewell.

Index

Note: *Italic* page numbers refer to figures.

For Product Safety Concerns and Information please contact our EU
representative GPSR@taylorandfrancis.com
Taylor & Francis Verlag GmbH, Kaufingerstraße 24, 80331 München, Germany

www.ingramcontent.com/pod-product-compliance
Ingram Content Group UK Ltd.
Pitfield, Milton Keynes, MK11 3LW, UK
UKHW051054080625
459435UK00010B/73

9781032419411